STEPPING UP AND STEPPING OUT

LIVING YOUR FAITH
RIGHT WHERE YOU ARE

The Remarkable Story of Garry Kinder
and the Bent Tree Bible Study

Lu Ann Fowler

insight publishing group
Tulsa, Oklahoma

STEPPING UP AND STEPPING OUT

Stepping Up and Stepping Out by Lu Ann Fowler
Published by Insight Publishing Group
8801 S. Yale, Suite 410
Tulsa, OK 74137
918-493-1718

Unless otherwise indicated, Scripture quotations are from the *Holy Bible, The King James Version.* Other quotations are from the *New International Version (NIV).* Copyright 1973, 1978, 1984 International Bible Society. Used by permission of Zondervan Bible Publishers.

2nd Printing
9000 books in print

ISBN: 1-930027-79-6
Library of Congress catalog card number: 2002115424
Printed in the United States of America

ENDORSEMENTS

Garry Kinder is one of the finest churchmen I have ever had the privilege of knowing. His Sunday morning Bent Tree Bible Study is one of the most innovative ministries anywhere in the world. This layman's commitment to the Word of God, to ministry and to people, causes the Church in our day to blush. You will be challenged and changed when you read this phenomenal account of how one of America's leading businessmen has committed his life to fulfilling the Great Commission.

Dr. Mac Brunson
Senior Pastor
First Baptist Dallas

When I got the manuscript, I did not put it down until I finished reading it completely. Reading these pages will cause anyone to feel they know Garry and want to share his commitment to Christ. Pick it up. Read it. When you put it down, you will be better for having walked its pages and known its people.

Dr. Richard Jackson
Pastor Emeritus
North Phoenix Baptist Church

Stepping Up and Stepping Out is more than the title of this great volume, it is the theme of Garry Kinder's life and experience. Courage, integrity and faithfulness mark this remarkable man's life. Those same qualities mark this book. What a blessing!!

John A. Weber
Chaplain
Dallas Cowboys

Garry Kinder has always been a person who has stepped up and stepped out. He has done it with the Fellowship of Christian Athletes, Bent Tree Bible Study and the Roaring Lambs Organization. This book will inspire you to live your faith on a daily basis.

Roger Staubach
Hall of Fame Quarterback
Founder, The Staubach Company

This book is a must read for any Christian wondering how to share their faith. It is a unique story of a man who started a Bible study to teach for ten weeks, and instead started an extraordinary ministry that has lasted over twenty-two years.

Dennis McClain
Chief Executive Officer
Temerlin McClain

Read and learn from this high–energy, intelligent, positive, God-fearing man with whom I've worked for forty-five years. What he's taught the Bent Tree Bible Study, Diane and me is now available to the world.

Dr. Ken Miller
Former President
Grand Canyon University Foundation

Garry Kinder shows that it is not only what you say, but also what you do that counts in life. Garry is a man whose every area of life reflects what he believes and teaches at Bent Tree Bible Study. Read and learn from a man who "walks the talk."

James K. Dahlgren
President
Dahlgren Duck, Inc.

As a close friend of Garry's, I've cheered for him in his many mountaintop experiences, as he did for me in our championship years with the Cleveland Browns. We've also walked through hard times and discovered that they weren't volcanoes to destroy us, but valleys to strengthen us. There are no friends like old friends. Garry is one of my very best friends. This book reveals secrets of his highly victorious life!

Bill Glass
Founder & Evangelist
Champions for Life (formerly Bill Glass Ministries)

Under Garry's leadership, the Bent Tree Bible Study has had an overwhelming influence on many, many individuals and families. The pages of this book will give you a way to pattern your daily walk through life. It will inspire you to follow God's nudges to influence others for the glory of His Kingdom.

Gary Newell
Insurance Broker
Lifelong Friend

For thirty years Garry Kinder has been a friend and an inspiration. Garry has been a role model for all who have aspired to succeed while striving to do it the right way. Ethics and moral values, combined with knowledge and enthusiasm, have always put him in front of the pack in everything he has done. This latest book, *Stepping Up and Stepping Out,* is inspirational and motivational. Lives have been changed as Garry taught and lived the contents of this book and will continue to do so through the book's longevity.

Grant Teaff
Executive Director
American Football Coaches Association

The Bent Tree Bible Study is a living example of what God can do with a man who is devoted to Christ and determined to share his faith with others. The man is Garry Kinder and the Bible study is one of the most effective ministries in Dallas for the past two decades. This compelling story will challenge readers to begin fulfilling God's mission for their lives. I absolutely love this book!

Dr. Jack Graham
Pastor
Prestonwood Baptist Church

Among the many Bible studies Garry has started and taught himself, he helped me start a Bible study for the Dallas Cowboy players and coaches with Dr. Howard Hendricks and Dr. Tony Evans as teachers in the early years — a Bible study that continues to have a great impact on players and community alike. Garry quickly became a dear and trusted friend.

Bill Krisher
Western Divisional Vice President
Fellowship of Christian Athletes

DEDICATION

This book is dedicated to Tommie H. Dodrill and Avis M. Dodrill, parents of Greg Dodrill. It is through their inspiration and financial support that this book is possible.

This book is also dedicated to the many participants and friends of Bent Tree Bible Study who have proven on a daily basis that they are willing to *"step up and step out"* for the cause of Christ.

TABLE OF CONTENTS

Part IV
THE REST OF THE STORY . . .

Part V
FIGURATIVELY TAPPED ON THE SHOULDER . . . JUST DO IT!

ACKNOWLEDGMENTS

Jack and Garry Kinder have been my employers for over twenty-two years at Kinder Brothers International (KBI). During that time I have become involved in the business as an executive assistant. Watching their children and grandchildren grow up has been very helpful to my family and me.

It was in the early stages of my employment at KBI, that the Bent Tree Bible Study came into existence. I have enjoyed participating in their programs on several occasions. Rick and Jan Loy are longtime friends, whom I highly respect. It was exciting to watch the creation of the Bent Tree Counseling Center, which now sees hundreds of clients each month. I also watched the inception of the Roaring Lambs Organization and saw how God led John and Billie Gillespie to move to Dallas and take over the leadership of that dynamic program.

It was a thrill for me to be asked to be involved in the writing of this book. A project of this nature cannot come about without the help of many people. First and foremost, I want to thank Helen Hosier who not only wrote the preface to the book, but was also instrumental in using her professional writing skills and advice on many occasions. She was also involved in the interviewing of many of the people who wrote their stories in this book. For years Helen has been known for her writing skills and has currently authored a book on grandparenting.

Janet and Garry Kinder were very helpful in reviewing the written material, verifying its accuracy. Rick and Jan Loy's contribution regarding the history of Bent Tree Bible Study has been invaluable. Anton and Donna Skell were very instrumental in many of the stories and testimonies along the way, matching the pictures with the story line.

Thanks to John Gillespie for his help with the Roaring Lambs story. Karol Kinder Ladd and Karen Kinder Smith, Garry's daughters, were involved in writing many of the chapters throughout the book. I'm thankful to Kathy Golla, Bill Glass and Evelyn Hinds for their contributions.

I appreciate Dr. O.S. Hawkins writing the introduction. His spiritual leadership and advice has been very helpful to Garry over the years, especially as the Roaring Lambs organization began to grow.

These are examples of people who are *Stepping Up and Stepping Out.*

Lu Ann Fowler
Author

INTRODUCTION

What can one man do? Ask Moses. One man can be used of God to deliver a nation. Ask Nehemiah. One man, moved by God's Spirit, can be used to not only rebuild a wall, but also a hope when it was almost gone. What can one man do? Ask Garry Kinder. One man can influence a multitude of men and women.

We derive our word "influence" from a Latin word that means "in flow." The word picture is that of a small stream that flows into a larger river and gets carried away and caught up in its flow. *Stepping Up and Stepping Out* is the story of hundreds of people who have been caught up in Garry's flow.

The Psalmist said, "The steps of a good man are ordered by the Lord; and He delights in his way" (Psalm 37:23). Garry has taught us all to not simply step up and step out, but to "step over." Down through the years we have watched him as he has "stepped over" one obstacle, heartbreak, or difficulty after another. On the anvil of personal experience he has beaten out these time-tested and God-honoring truths of the Christian life. His life matches the lessons of his lips.

He has also taught us by example to "step down." A lot of teachers stay up on the pedestal as it were. Garry Kinder steps down to walk with us not simply to talk to us. His humble spirit and servant heart speak louder than all his words of wisdom combined.

Garry has also taught us to "step in." He has stepped into our hearts and modeled before us the tremendous truth that life is about relationships. Those of us "in Christ" are closer related to one another than to our own blood relatives who do not know Him.

The Kinder brothers are the original dynamic duo. Personally, I trust I will always prove worthy of their love, encouragement and friendship. Thank you Garry, for stepping up and stepping out and doing so "with the integrity of your heart and the skillfulness of your hands" (Psalm 78:72). We are caught up in your flow.

O.S. Hawkins
President/CEO
Southern Baptist Convention Annuity Board
Dallas, Texas

PREFACE

by Helen Hosier

*If we do not radiate the light of Christ around us, the sense of
the darkness that prevails in the world will increase.*

Mother Teresa in *One Heart Full of Love*[1]

THE LIGHT THAT
LIGHTETH EVERY MAN

*In him was life; and the life was the light of men.
And the light shineth in darkness; and the darkness
comprehended it not...That was the true Light,
which lighteth every man that cometh into the world.*
John 1:4, 5, 9

"I have an invitation to a Christmas open house," I told a
friend. "Will you go with me?" She was delighted and responded enthusiastically. A couple of weeks later we were on our way.

Cars were parked up and down the street and, in the middle of the block, to our left, cars were entering the circular drive
in front of a home festooned with sparkling white lights. People
were stepping out of the cars and pausing to look at a brightly
lit sign. "Look at that sign!" my friend exclaimed.

It stood there, a beautiful 4 by 8 foot sign, giving the
appearance of a parchment scroll with Old English lettering pro-
claiming "Jesus is the Light of the world" (John 8:12). A spotlight
strategically focused on a star poised above the wording caught
our attention.

"No mistaking that this is the place," I responded.

All the homes on the street were magnificently decorated,
but this was special — special in its dignity and beauty proclaim-

ing the truth of the reason for the season. "This is going to be a lovely evening," I said to my friend. "December 1, what a perfect way to begin the holidays."

Light poured from the front door as we entered and were greeted by other guests. A quick glance revealed candlelight coming from every direction, warm and welcoming. Stepping into the light I noticed my friend Evelyn across the room and slightly to the right. She waved and made her way to us and snapped our photo. "You are the official photographer I gather," I said as I introduced her to my friend Karolyn.

"The food is to your left," she directed, as the three of us made small talk. "Have a wonderful time," she added as she got ready to snap someone else's picture.

The smell of food beckoned and we made our way through the guests to the attractively decorated dining room table. "Beverages are around the corner," the server told us.

The sound of Christmas music filled the air and we observed the pianist, Judy Moore Bird, at the keyboard and the bass fiddler, Gil Pitts. The twinkling lights on the Christmas tree, the fire in the fireplace, the men and women mingling and engaged in animated conversation, a couple of darling little girls darting across the hall in their pretty dresses—it was all very festive and delightful; a perfect setting for a party.

"So glad you are here, welcome." It was Garry, the host. He patted my arm, "And who is this?" he asked, and introductions were made. His smile lit up his face. "Janet is over there," he motioned, and I noticed the light reflecting on her lovely face. She was surrounded by smiling faces. To myself I thought: *There is so much shining light here* ... and I mentioned this to my friend as we found a comfortable place to sit and enjoy our refreshments. Light radiated from every place in the house and the guests seemed wrapped in warm embracing light. Glancing across the room, into the foyer, on a carved breakfront, I saw candlelight reflecting on the faces of Mary, Joseph, the shepherds, and the Baby lying in the manger.

"This open house is an annual event," I told my friend. "People who have attended the Bent Tree Bible Study class are invited."

"I'm anxious to learn about this Garry and Janet and this class," my friend said. "You will," I smiled at her. "I promise. Trust me. This is a wonderful story."

At the end of every lesson at Bent Tree Bible Study, Garry Kinder leaves the class with "What We Learned." I'd like to leave you with these thoughts, which are the message of this book and our purpose as Believers in Christ.

> God through the dark hath set the Light of life,
> With witness for Himself, the Word of God,
> To be among us Man, with human heart,
> And human language, thus interpreting
> The One great Will incomprehensible,
> Only so far as we in human life
> Are able to receive it.
>
> Oswald Chambers[2]

WHAT WE LEARNED

☐ Jesus is the Light of the World.

☐ Come to the Light.

☐ Step up, step out, and bring others to the Light.

Part I

A Nudge from God

ONE

It's no secret. The ministry of the Church is a genuine concern for others. We need to stop talking about it and start doing it. Rise and shine, friend. Everyone you meet today is on heaven's "Most Wanted" list.

Charles R. Swindoll in *Rise & Shine: A Wake-up Call*[1]

BELLY UP TO THE BAR

*Go out unto the highways and hedges,
and compel them to come in.*
Luke 14:23

Unconventional. Interdenominational. Unpressured. These are words that describe what's been happening for more than twenty years at a country club in Dallas, Texas on Sunday mornings at 9:15 A.M. As more than one observer said at the outset, "Just belly up to the bar and have some coffee and Danish along with a Bible study." Bloody Marys and hors d'oeuvres were not featured. The year was 1980, the Bent Tree Country Club was the place and Garry Kinder was the teacher.

By the time the *Dallas Morning News* caught on to what was happening at the posh country club, the Sunday morning class had attracted well-known athletes and musicians, along with businessmen and women, neighbors whose homes surrounded the Bent Tree Country Club, and others coming from the Metroplex. One visitor to the class expressed surprise that a successful businessman would give of his time to the Lord in a country club setting like this. When Evelyn Hinds was invited to participate on a Sunday morning and she encountered Garry Kinder for the first time, she said to him, "Oh, you're the pastor."

Always quick to set the record straight when people refer to him as a pastor, Garry Kinder responded, "No, I'm not a pastor." Then what is he? A layman. A professional speaker and co-founder of an internationally recognized management consulting firm, Kinder Brothers International, Inc., based in Dallas. A layman, who responded to a suggestion from Billy Weber, then pastor of Prestonwood Baptist Church, that he teach a class for ten weeks. They wanted to see if there would be interest among individuals in the community for an hour-long Bible study on Sunday mornings away from a church.

"We weren't given the Gospel just to keep to ourselves. It's too good to do that," Garry says. With a quiet determination and humble passion, he accepted the challenge. Obviously needs were being met and today the Bent Tree Bible Study (BTBS), still going strong, can look back on more than twenty-two years of meeting every Sunday morning.

Polo Player Comes to Christ

In 1983 Bill Conley was a polo player with the Willow Bend Polo and Hunt Club. Bill recounts, "One day at the Polo Club, Buzz Welker invited me to go to a Bible study that met in the bar at the Bent Tree Country Club. I told him I didn't go to things like that. (I had given up on church.) Back then I spent a lot of time in that bar though. Buzz said 'You're there the night before, all you need to do is show up there in the morning.' I thought about it and I decided I would."

That decision started Bill on a spiritual journey that soon led him to a decision to become a follower of Christ. "I connected with Garry because he is a businessman and so am I. My salvation was a direct result of Garry's teaching at the Bible study."

Looking back at his spiritual history Bill remembers, "as a child growing up my family attended church regularly. At the age of twelve I was offered the opportunity to be confirmed. That was the process then in the Methodist church. My parents encouraged me but did not pressure me in this process. This is a fact that I have always appreciated.

"After becoming an adult, I associated myself with another traditional church denomination. While never becoming a

Christian, this is what started me on the road to disassociating myself with the church life. As I looked for older male role models in the church, what I found were men that were one person on Sunday and a totally different person the balance of the week. This hypocrisy is what eventually divided me from the church.

"It was at BTBS and through the leadership and example of Garry Kinder in the fall of 1983 that I came to know and surrender my life to Jesus as my Lord and Savior. That was the beginning of a life-changing path for me. Over the period of the next years the Lord worked in my life to clean up areas of sin. *The thing that Garry has always stressed that made a difference in my leadership role in my own family is that children do not learn from what you say but what you do.*

"My personal core values are integrity, commitment, and caring. These are core values that are regularly taught and lived out by Garry. Because of his commitment to me, I have a stronger family; I apply leadership skills in my daily life that I have learned at the Bible study. I am wholly committed to serving God, which makes me excited about living every day. I may not have taken the time to properly thank Garry, but he has certainly impacted my life!"

Bill Conley and his family continue to be regular members at the Bible study nearly twenty years later. Bill was just one of the people that was targeted when Garry started a Bible study in a bar . . . those that may not want to go to a church.

As the size of the class increased, they eventually moved from the bar at the Bent Tree Country Club into a larger room. Outgrowing that room after six years, they then moved to the Prestonwood Country Club where they've been meeting since 1987.

This innovative approach is a means to reach people who shy away from the traditional church setting. As for the barroom atmosphere, Dr. Weber, in an interview with the Dallas paper said, "We laugh about it a lot, but we're not offended wherever we teach. The place still has people with needs in their lives.

"Sunday is, [for many people], a day of recreation. So we say, that's all right. Go play your golf or your tennis, but stop off for Bible study on the way." There were some who dropped in wearing golf shirts and shorts, in tennis gear, but as time progressed, as the class was taken through the Bible, and as the teacher suggested from time to time that they go on to a church of their choice, some people began arriving dressed for attendance at a worship service elsewhere.

Part of the attraction of the class is the easy-going atmosphere. One man explained it like this: "We start on time and end on time, and you can come casual or in a suit. When we invite someone we run around with during the week, we are comfortable with what we know will take place, and we can say, 'The teacher is not a minister; he's a highly respected, successful businessman who teaches in a great conversational style.' That has real appeal. There is no roll call, no membership list, they don't get on your case, and they don't take offerings or mention finances."

Linda Ann Blakely came from Virginia to Dallas in 1979. When she heard of the Bent Tree Bible Study, she decided to give it a try. "I wasn't going to any church or Bible study, in fact, in Virginia I had already started slacking off. It bothered me, so I was quite intrigued when I heard about this group meeting in a bar. I started attending once a month, then twice a month, and before I knew it, I was going four times a month and didn't want to miss. I really took to heart what Garry was saying. He was a very good Bible teacher. I was learning so much. I found the more I read the Bible, the more I wanted to study it, and the closer I got to God. The closer you get to God, the greater you find His love, and you want more and more. I came back to the Lord because of this class and Garry's teachings. I've been coming for more than twenty-two years."

Dr. Jack Graham, popular pastor of the Prestonwood Baptist Church (an ever-growing Dallas church), in speaking at a Roaring Lambs Hall of Fame breakfast early in 2002, spoke of the Bent Tree Bible Study class as "a cutting-edge ministry," and that "extreme days demand extreme Christians." He pointed to the need for Christians to get out of "their comfort zones" and into the culture with the Gospel message.

Garry Kinder knew that when God taps you on the shoulder to do something for Him, He equips you to get the job done.

Sensing that this was that kind of a God-nudge, he stepped out in obedience. He had already learned the principle that the will of God will never take you where the grace of God cannot keep you, and his response was a ready willingness to be used of God. What was to happen in the years ahead he had no way of knowing, but Garry knew that God knew.

WHAT WE LEARNED

☐ Every person is important to God and His plan for reaching the world with the good news of the Gospel.

☐ It's not our ability but our availability. God will empower us to do what He wants us to do. God does not call the qualified; He qualifies the called.

☐ Be sensitive to the nudges of God and step out in obedience. God always honors obedience.

What I Learned

_____
_____
_____
_____
_____
_____
_____
_____
_____
_____
_____
_____

I'll Walk It Out By . . .

_____
_____
_____
_____
_____
_____
_____
_____
_____
_____
_____
_____
_____
_____

TWO

We live and minister in a society that is pervasively and constantly changing, but eternal verities must not be compromised. In other words, we must determine what cannot change and what must change. Knowing the difference enables us to progress, because knowing what should not change releases us to be open to alternatives in other areas. Values and practices must be aligned.

Dr. Howard Hendricks in *Color Outside the Lines:*
A Revolutionary Approach to Creative Leadership[1]

COSMOPOLITAN AND COMFORTABLE

Now we believe…
John 4:42

Origins and beginnings of businesses, ministries, successful enterprises and the involvement of individuals are always interesting. We like stories. Everyone has a story or stories in them. James W. Barrie said that the life of every man is a diary in which he means to write one story and writes another, and his humblest hour too often is when he compares the volume as it is with what he intended to make it. It's a powerful thought and will set one's mind to thinking. Many people upon reading that will find themselves with some regrets; others will feel motivated to make some changes to chart a new course for their life. Still others can look back upon their "volume" and feel gratitude that their story has turned out the way they hoped it would — with God doing more than they ever imagined possible.

The story of Bent Tree Bible Study is one such story. *There are people who heard the challenge and felt called to be part of whatever was going to take place.* Some of those people became a part of the initial formation group and are actively involved today. These are people who *"stepped up and stepped out."*

When Billy Weber threw down the gauntlet to a group of leaders of a monthly breakfast meeting of Christian business-men and women meeting at Bent Tree Country Club, he challenged them to recognize the need to reach out. The group was called the North Dallas Christian Fellowship Breakfast.

Once a month they would bring in an inspirational speaker who would communicate the business principles that helped make him successful and then give a personal testimony. As Billy spoke to the core group of men and women involved in that outreach, he said, "Not everyone is comfortable coming to a church.

"There are people from every imaginable background who need to be introduced to what the Bible has to say. Some of them have never darkened the doors of a church. Others may have drifted away from church attendance—you'll find Baptists, Lutherans, Presbyterians, Jews, Catholics and Muslims. Some have no denominational preference. How are they going to hear the Truth? What is being done to reach out to them? I am convinced that it needs to be a layman who leads such a Bible study and I've asked Garry Kinder to consider doing that. As you all know, Garry is a professional speaker—and very convincing and good at what he does—so I think it would work. But it will take the help of people like you."

"An organizational meeting was held in the home of Bobby Burns," Garry recalls. "Some of the people in that core group were Mary Kay Ash, Anton and Donna Skell, Bob and Shirley Bobbitt, Loma and Neva Allen, Lawson and Fran Ridgway, Ray and Kit Smith, Chuck and Carol Hamilton, J.D. and Mary Jane Phillips, and Morris and Mary Francis West. That evening, during the fellowship, Billy encouraged me to give the group a taste of how we would teach the Bible study. We did this with a fifteen-minute study of the life of the Apostle Peter. Two weeks later we met for the first time at the Cosmopolitan Lady Fitness Club owned by Anton and Donna Skell."

"Donna and I had never really studied the Bible together," Anton recalls. "Donna came from a Jewish background, and I was Presbyterian. We thought it would be perfect for us." The Skells were truly representative of exactly the kind of people Weber had in mind. After discussing it together and then with Weber and Garry Kinder, the decision was made to start at the Cosmopolitan Club, which was closed on Sundays. "We can bring out the folding chairs and Garry, you can bring the lesson," they said.

Garry's daughters, Karen Smith and Karol Ladd, remember helping to set up the chairs at the Cosmopolitan Club. "Anton and Donna played such an important role in the beginning and they still do today," Karol recalls. "They have been so instrumental in helping to maintain the strength of the Bible study."

Donna laughingly recalls, "We committed the ultimate sin. We took the exercise cards out of the bins and filled them with donuts." Their club was located across from the then, well-known Prestonwood Mall. Dallasites knew the area well. On a Sunday morning in 1980 with steaming cups of coffee and donuts, Anton and Donna Skell, Garry and Barbara Kinder, their daughters, and others greeted the first participants of what God knew was to be a long and fruitful "cutting edge" ministry.

A Venture of Faith

And come they did. The old maxim, "find a need and fill it," worked even in a venture such as this. It was really a venture of faith.

Garry had made the decision to teach from the beginning of the Bible, Genesis, and go right straight through. "Line by line, he taught us," Donna explains. "It's the best way to become acquainted with the Bible and to grow spiritually because you retain those Scriptures when you go through them like that." He took his cue from the late Dr. W. A. Criswell, the well-known and greatly respected pastor of the large downtown First Baptist Church of Dallas, where Garry and his family were members.

It was Criswell's method of preaching and it attracted thousands every Sunday. Garry had been well taught. Not only had he benefited for years under the teachings of Dr. Criswell, but he also sat in Mrs. Criswell's Sunday school class for ten years. Her reputation as a Bible teacher saw hundreds coming Sunday after Sunday, year after year. Garry had the blessing, prayers and interest of the Criswells and the people of the church. Fortified by such strong backing, and confident that God was in this effort of their getting out of the box and reaching into the community of the unchurched, Garry and several couples, including the Skells, stepped out.

Anton and Donna were excited to be part of the Bent Tree Bible Study. "The Country Club was not going to be available for ten weeks, but we were ready to start. That's when we decided to meet in the Aerobics Room at the Fitness Club." They and others started promoting the class through the North Dallas Christian Fellowship Breakfast, through their businesses, to their friends and neighbors. They soon realized that the class would minister to all kinds of people — those who hadn't found a church yet, weren't part of a specific denomination, or hadn't ever been part of a Bible study. New singles and widows who did not want to attend a singles' class were attracted to this study comprised of all ages, backgrounds, and levels of personal spiritual growth.

People in difficult situations found the anonymity of the class comfortable. *The nature and purpose of the class was to help them understand and apply the Scriptures to their daily living, believing that they would grow spiritually and eventually funnel into churches.* "We never were meant to replace a church, so regular attendance was not a factor. It just started as a ten-week Bible study that grew and everyone wanted it to continue. The Fitness Club was definitely not 'churchy' and people felt very comfortable in coming."

Donna remembered that it wasn't the kind of Bible study where you had to know the Bible to flip to something. "We were all on the same page and going through it together, chapter by chapter, verse by verse. There were no uncomfortable feelings of not knowing. People weren't asked questions, they weren't asked to pray aloud, there was nothing intimidating for anyone.

"I had been through the Old Testament since I'm Jewish, but never as a Christian. I didn't think there were a lot of references to Jesus Christ in the Old Testament, but after sitting under Garry's teachings I learned otherwise. It was really exciting for me when he started on the first page of Genesis. Since those first studies, as a group we've been through the entire Bible twice, and at the outset of 2002 we started going through it for the third time.

"Raising money has never been a key issue. We've always had enough money for the class to launch other ministries such as the Bent Tree Counseling Center [more on that in chapter eight], and Roaring Lambs.org. [See chapter thirteen.] There has been an emphasis towards reaching businesspeople. Garry is good at presenting business values and principles from the Bible that fit right in with what he's teaching on any given Sunday. It's been a very effective approach, a unique way of spreading what the Bible says and being creative about it. *There is a strong emphasis on how to apply the Bible to everyday life.* Each week Garry closes the class by saying, *'What three things did you learn today?'* These are nuggets of God's truth the people can take with them.

"It's so good to sit there and hear what the people say. They may not remember the exact scripture verses or the historical background and significance of the material, but they do leave with truths that they are going to apply in their lives for positive, Christ-like change. Seeing peoples' lives change keeps us motivated to continue accepting the challenge of *"stepping up and stepping out"* when God asks us to, again and again.

"What's so good about how it's done is that it's so easy to invite someone to come. Now we have attractive plastic cards, like a calling card, and you can tell someone about the class and hand them the card. It shows our vital statistics: time, location, office address, phone numbers. And the key statement on the card is: **'Applying the Bible to Everyday Living!'** When you say that it's taught by a businessman who is a motivational speaker by profession, and that he teaches the Bible with the same enthusiasm, you will see people's eyes light up and you know you have their attention. Thousands of people have come to the class that way, just by word of mouth."

On the occasion of the fifteenth anniversary of the Bent Tree Bible Study in 1995, as a tribute to Garry Kinder, Donna

Skell reminisced, *"I've figured it out. I learned three things each week, multiplied times fifteen years. So, you've blessed me with 2,250 life-changing thoughts. . . .* If I had to sum it all up, the three most important things I've learned from you, Garry, and from your teaching, are:

☐ First, that without a doubt, the Bible is the inspired Word of God. It is unique in its way to minister to all of us; it has answers to every question we could ask; it has comfort; and it is well worth studying every day of our lives.

☐ The second thing I've learned is that Jesus Christ is the answer to all of our needs.

☐ And the third thing I've learned from you is 'Now go and tell others'."

She closed by saying, "Thank You, God, for using Garry to share Your truth with me."

WHAT WE LEARNED

☐ Everyone has a story. Resolve to "write" the story of your life, with God's help, in such a way that you will have as few regrets as possible.

☐ Step out in faith for God. "Find a need and fill it."

☐ The Word of God is changeless. It has power to change lives, including mine.

Success Guideposts for Life!

(found on the back of the calling card mentioned in this chapter)

Start early each day!

Make it a habit to eat with the early crowd each morning. Stay energetic by scheduling a rigorous 30-minute work-out each day.

Use your gifts, abilities and energies on fruitful pursuits!

Choose the important things to be done, and do them to the very best of your abilities. Make every occasion a great occasion.

Character building comes before all!

Keep your mind, body and spirit clean. Keep good, encouraging company. Fill your mind with positive and productive thoughts.

Commitment is the key to any successful endeavor!

Stick to your tasks, keep your promises and fulfill your commitments with excellence. Develop the ability to live in balance and "bounce back" from adversity.

Expect to excel!

Being thorough in preparation and diligent in application will make desirable things happen. Self-confidence comes from successful experiences.

Speak the truth with passion and compassion. Live it as you speak it.

Words are powerful, especially when they are supported by a life of constant integrity.

Stay close to God!

Do His will and keep His commandments. He is your greatest friend and protector. He has clearly demonstrated His love for you by offering new life and forgiveness through His Son, Jesus Christ. Believe in Him and trust in His ways always.

What I Learned

_____
_____
_____
_____
_____
_____
_____
_____
_____
_____
_____
_____

I'll Walk It Out By . . .

_____
_____
_____
_____
_____
_____
_____
_____
_____
_____
_____
_____
_____
_____

THREE

God wants the Holy Spirit to flow out of our hearts, not only for our blessing but so that we might be channels of blessing to others.

Jack Graham in *Lessons from the Heart*

GOD'S WORD SPOKEN— GOD'S PURPOSE ACCOMPLISHED

. . . so is My word that goes out from My mouth: It will not return to Me empty but will accomplish what I desire . . .
Isaiah 55:11

They came. Visitors to the Bent Tree Bible Study class came from all over the Metroplex, from all walks of life and all denominations. They were meeting in the bar at the Bent Tree Country Club. When *The Dallas Morning News* reported on the unusual setting, they said: "Next to the coffee cups, well-thumbed Bibles rest on the white cloth-covered bar tables. The eighty or so 'customers,' dressed in their Sunday best, clearly are here for inspiration, not recreation . . . The Bent Tree Bible Study class is the uptown, upper-class equivalent of street-corner preaching, an evangelical outreach to the wealthy in their habitat."

Commenting on that, Garry Kinder would tell you that "The up-and-outers need the Gospel just as much as down-and-outers." But they weren't then, nor are they today all "upper-class" people. There are singles—some raising children, some struggling to make ends meet. There are others whose lives have been disrupted by divorce. There are some seeking answers for the curves life has thrown them. There are those who know the pain of the death of a loved one.

The couples are a mixed blend of ages—handsome men and attractive women—most of whom appear successful. Some are retired, others in the prime of life still making their mark in their careers.

All who come value the warmth and love they find in fellowship with others learning more about God. They experience the truth that God's Word meets people right where they are, at the point of their need. Truly, people "come just as they are" and taste "living water."

God's Higher Ways

Jim Wolfe, who has attended since 1981, tells of a young woman who came to his home on a business-related matter. "After we completed our transaction, she asked where my wife and I attended church. I told her I was recently retired from the military and that we were looking for a church. We had visited a few but had not found the right one for us—we wanted clear teaching about what the Bible really says. She told me about Bent Tree Bible Study meeting in the country club bar and about Garry's down-to-earth teaching style. She said that the atmosphere was easygoing and that we would be welcomed there. Later, I spoke to my wife about it and explained the unique setting. She said, 'Well, having spent twenty-five years in the military, you've seen lots of bars, you should feel right at home there! Let's try it out.'

"The next Sunday morning we arrived a little before 9:15—and most of the chairs were full—but we found a place to sit. Garry started on time and finished on time. I appreciated that. We really enjoyed how Garry explained the way to apply the lesson of Scripture to our lives today. We visited a few more times and then made the decision to attend on a regular basis. *The interesting thing, though, is that I didn't see the lady who had originally invited us.* I wanted to introduce her to my wife. I wanted to thank her for the invitation and let her know just how much the teaching had come to mean to us. I kept thinking that the business connection would at least bring her back to purchase more products, but it did not. I finally came to the conclusion that it was definitely the Lord's will for us to attend Bent

Tree Bible Study, and He used the invitation of a stranger to make a difference in my life."

In the years that followed, both Jim's sweet wife and his precious son died. Like so many others who were attracted to the class, life continued to "happen", even after loss. Some of those life experiences were joyous, wonderful times; others brought incredible heartache and sorrow.

Learning to look to God's Word provides strength and comfort for the difficult times, and instruction for all of life. To this day, Jim is thankful for the young woman he has never seen again who pointed him to the place God wanted him to be. God continues to use His Word and the people of this Bible study in Jim's life.

Donna Skell speaks of the many answers to prayer—both the joyous and the difficult times. "We have celebrated weddings together—some of the singles in the class found new mates and we rejoiced with them. We have celebrated births—the births of children and grandchildren. We've had a lot of fun together, too. But there were also difficult times—the deaths of loved ones and the sorrow that accompanies loss. But we were always there for each other."

Around *The Family Table*

We never know what God might be up to when we gather around the table as a family. We can know one thing for sure: He's always working things out for good.

Patty McCrory, long-time member of the Bible study, shares what God has done in her family's life through studying His Word and prayer around *The Family Table*.

She recounts, "Martha Chamberlin invited me to the Super Bowl Breakfast, January, 1987. On the Sunday Tom Landry was guest speaker, I invited my brother, Tom Jessup, and when we walked in we saw our brother, John (he had been invited by a co-worker). Not long afterwards our sister, Elizabeth Miller, joined us. The four siblings, plus spouses, have become known as *The Family Table*. This Bible study has been a constant in my life over all these years and has provided not only fellowship and an insight into God's word, but also quality time with our family on a regular basis."

Patty not only feeds her spirit at Bent Tree Bible Study but she exercises her faith in her life. She was a widow when she first attended. Along the way, she brought her second husband, Don Griffin. He loved Garry and, under his teaching, Don grew in his faith. Don's untimely death was a shock and it was Garry Kinder and Rick Loy that Patty called on to conduct Don's memorial service.

Sometime later Diane Nowell, a friend from Bent Tree Bible Study, connected Patty with Bill McCrory. Patty tells that she had just started praying two weeks before for a husband who loved the Lord as much as she did and one with an Irish heritage and a lake home. (Garry teaches on the importance of praying specifically if you want a specific answer.) It took Bill seven months to call for the first date but when he did, another love story began and marriage followed.

Patty's third husband, Bill, continues the story. "Don Griffin was one of my best friends. I had seen the positive spiritual changes in him after he married Patty. That impressed me." Patty and Bill were married in 1994. Bill also became a regular at BTBS. Bill explains, "I was a new Believer back then. I always say I grew up at Bent Tree Bible Study. That is where I really got into the Bible." Patty and Bill regularly drive the sixty-five miles from their lake home at Cedar Creek Lake to attend the Bible study and also to make the family connections. They can often be seen leaving early so they can also attend the worship service at their Dallas church.

Tom Jessup, Elizabeth and W.O. Miller, Patty and Bill McCrory, and John and Sandra Jessup comprise the regulars at *The Family Table*. When their sister, Kathryn Maracin, is in town she attends as well. These siblings seem Texan through and through. Interestingly, their parents were immigrants.

"Mother was from Sweden and my dad was from Ireland," explains Patty. "They met in Minneapolis and moved to Texas in the 1930s. They both loved the Lord. Mother poured her life into her family. She wanted us to continue to be close and love the Lord." God answers prayers sometimes even after the pray-er has passed away. Elizabeth says "Mother would be so proud that we were meeting together like this on Sunday morning."

In May of 2002, Elizabeth and W.O.'s daughter-in-law, Lisa Owens Miller, spotted a vintage drum labeled Pekin High School in a Dallas antique shop. Since she had attended the Bible study many times she had heard Garry's frequent mention of his hometown. She called Elizabeth from her car phone and insisted that they should buy it for Garry.

The next Sunday Patty and Bill went directly to the shop after church to buy the drum on behalf of the siblings. During that transaction, dealers in the shop gathered around the cashier. They said they were curious to see who would buy that drum. "What in the world are you going to do with it?" they wondered. Always ready to say a good word on behalf of Bent Tree Bible Study and the Lord, Patty was delighted to explain the story. They took it home and Bill repaired the prize drum and tidied it up for the surprise to follow.

The sisters put their heads together to plan how they could present it to Garry. Elizabeth realized they would need drumsticks for effect. As she sat at her dining room table with the phone book open to find a music store, her son, Bruce, walked in and asked what she was doing. She explained and he told her to call Williamson Music Company, owned by a high school friend, Mark Williamson. "Tell him you're Thunder Miller's mother." She did and Mark became enthused after hearing the story and not only loaned the drumsticks but personally delivered them to the Miller home.

The Sunday following Garry's May 22 birthday was the day the family gathered outside the ballroom to enter with the present. They marched in beating the drum and singing "When the Saints Go Marching In." Rick Loy was in on the surprise and played his tape of Louis Armstrong's version of that hymn to accompany the parade.

Everyone was surprised and Garry was "beside himself" seeing the drum, an authentic piece of Americana from his hometown in Illinois. Janet Kinder reports that she and Garry took it to show his brother Jack that same afternoon. One wonders how that old drum made its way to Dallas and caught the sharp eye of someone who could put it in the hands of someone who would remember its heyday of years ago. If drums could talk. . . .

Looking at these stories from *The Family Table* the evidence of answered prayers abounds. As busy as life is for everyone, these family members make it a priority to meet every Sunday and that meeting encourages the other desire of their mother, "to love the Lord."

Patty reflects, "Garry's life, more than anything, has been a source of strength for me. He lives what he teaches and the discipline, integrity and commitment to doing his best shines through. He also teaches us that we should leave a legacy. Our mother's legacy is sitting around *The Family Table*.

Although her life has undergone a lot of changes over the past fifteen years, Patty McCrory remains a regular at Bent Tree Bible Study.

Love Blossoms

One couple, Brad and Tracy Popoff, refer to Kinder's ministry as being "instrumental in our spiritual walk." Brad said, "Garry impacted the very beginning of our relationship and eventually our marriage. At a church leadership retreat we were asked to write down a person's name who had affected our life in a significant way for good, and to list the qualities we admired in this person and the qualities we gained from this person. I had never really consciously thought about the impact Garry made on my life, but that night his name went down on my paper." In writing to Garry about this, Brad Popoff said: "Praise God for the way that you allow Him to speak through you. You speak with such a passion and love. Your drive is contagious to those around you."

Tracy Popoff recalls being brought to the Bible study through the invitation of two women—Diane Johnson and Donna Skell. She wrote to Garry: "I was just an infant in Christ. God's timing is so perfect. Sundays became the highlight of my week as God revealed Himself to me through studying the Scriptures through your teaching. For the first time in my life I saw and felt God's love through people who truly loved Him and lived out their faith. That time spent with all of you study-ing the Word, and the friendships that I enjoyed, was the turn-ing point in my life. It was a time of divine encounter. Thank you for the solid foundation of biblical teaching that I received that caused me to grow in my faith. I applaud your dedication to serving God and serving others."

I Am the Vine, You Are the *Branches*

The Bent Tree Bible Study's newsletter, *Branches*, includes stories about class members like these in this chapter. Evelyn Hinds, a member of the class puts together "life stories" about members of the class and includes them in the newsletter as one way of getting to know the other members of the "family" and how God is working in their lives. The newsletter can be found on the Bible study's Web site at: www.btbs.com.

The people of Bent Tree Bible Study have extended their own love and the love of God to each other. *They continue to allow the Holy Spirit to flow out of them to bless others.* The foundation for being able to bless others is the Word of God—then taking God at His Word and acting on it. His Word will not return to Him before it has accomplished His divine purpose.

"The unfolding of your words gives light;
it gives understanding to the simple."
Psalm 119:130

"Your word is a lamp to my feet
and a light for my path."
Psalm 119:105

"I will instruct you and teach you in
the way you should go; I will counsel
you and watch over you."
Psalm 32:8

What We Learned

☐ God's Word meets people where they are, according to their individual need.

☐ God uses willing people as His instruments to accomplish His purpose.

☐ God wants to use us to bless others.

What I Learned

_____

_____

_____

_____

_____

_____

_____

_____

_____

_____

_____

I'll Walk It Out By . . .

_____

_____

_____

_____

_____

_____

_____

_____

_____

_____

_____

FOUR

. . . CENTERED AND GROUNDED

That which we have seen and heard declare we unto you, that
ye also may have fellowship with us; and truly our fellowship is
with the Father, and with His Son, Jesus Christ.
1 John 1:3

L ives were being touched—deeply touched and changed.
Growth of the class forced them out of the Bent Tree
Country Club Bar into a larger room. Eventually, a place had to
be found that could accommodate the large number of people
who were dropping by. Many came out of curiosity but returned
out of a conviction that they needed what was being taught. The
nearby Prestonwood Country Club had a large ballroom that
proved to be the perfect facility to meet the class' ever-expand-
ing needs. It continues to meet there today.

One woman, perhaps quite representative of many who
were attending, explained her reasons for coming: "I was in a
very hurtful situation when I became a part of the class. My
sweet husband had died an untimely death in an automobile
accident and the ministers I turned to for consolation and guidance seemed to be falling one by one. To make the matter even
worse, one of my best friends became involved with one of the
ministers giving me a double disillusionment. It was a difficult
time and my faith was being tested.

"I found what I needed in the class—good, sound, biblical teaching—and it helped me a great deal. *It kept me centered and grounded.*"

A Place to Belong

One person spoke of his need to find "a place to worship and where I could belong." The love of the people in the class enabled him to say, "I found that place. We cannot help but be caught up in Garry's enthusiasm, bright smile, and loving arms of friendship. They say laughter sets the spirit free to move—and Garry supplies plenty of that! Walls that block communication don't have to be torn down because Garry doesn't allow them to be built in the first place. He teaches that we must reach down to help—and reach up when we need to be helped. It is then that we realize the extent of our need for one another and the Lord. One of the things Garry has taught us is that 'the greatest thing we can do as our faith grows and stretches is to share it with others.'"

Faithfulness

"Your faithful contribution to the Bent Tree Bible Study has been a constant source of inspiration through the good, as well as, the difficult times," an appreciative member expressed.

The sacrificial giving of his time, "contagious energy" and "tireless devotion" did not go unnoticed by class attendees. "An example of faithfulness, a mentor, and inspiration" were words that consistently showed up in conversations and letters from those who wanted to acknowledge what the class and Garry's teaching meant to them. Dedication to biblical precepts were acknowledged as hallmark traits of their teacher—a living out of what the Bible teaches that the followers of Jesus are to exemplify in their daily walk.

Ed and Nancy Arnold began attending the class in 1992. "We've been through the Bible with him one time and look forward to doing it again and again. The teaching of God's Word and the class have made a difference in our lives."Successful businesspeople, well-traveled, and knowledgeable about good business practices and world events, the Arnolds are representative of those who particularly recognize and value Garry's leadership and sharp business mind.

Many spoke of the manner in which Bible truths were made applicable to their daily lives. "It is not often you can find a teacher who can help you with your daily walk. Garry encourages us to read the Bible, taking special note of the practical help to be found in the book of Proverbs. He teaches us to pray specifically for needs, and to trust the Lord to answer our prayers in the way He knows is best for us. We have been greatly helped in our Christian walk."

The Biblical Message Made Vital and Personal

"The message of the Bible is vital and personal through your dynamic teaching. We have been strengthened and our faith grows stronger." A note such as this fuels the fire that burns in Garry as he responds to the leading of the Holy Spirit in the preparation of the lessons each Sunday.

One young admirer wrote, "Your lifestyle has been a blessing to everyone, especially me. Thank you for your spiritual leadership, your guidance and your influence on my life."

In the earlier years of the class, children were ministered to also—as one woman recalls "in a room across the hall"—while their parents sat under Garry's teaching. Teenagers and young college students attended and participated with their parents. "Our youngest daughter was just fourteen when we were still meeting in the Bent Tree Bar. I know the lessons she learned in the class are going to make her a better lawyer," a mother wrote. Parents told me their sons and daughters benefited greatly from the teachings, time and interest Garry invested in speaking to their young adults. "You can be proud of the honest, Christian young man our son is today," one woman's letter stated. She gave credit to the teachings her son absorbed in the Bible study class.

Proud for those parents, yes, but humbled, Garry is reminded of what *stepping out* and taking that initial risk in accepting the recommendation that he become teacher for such a class has actually meant. God continues to bring people to BTBS that need someone to reach down to help them. Through the power of His Word, people are given the courage to reach up to be helped. *When God uses you to help others, it's a very humbling experience—it intensifies that burning to "walk humbly with our God."*

When you enroll in the "school of faith," you never know what may happen next. . . . The life of faith presents challenges that keep you going—and keep you growing.

Warren W. Wiersbe in *Be Obedient*[1]

WHAT WE LEARNED

☐ The greatest thing we can do as our faith grows and stretches is to share it with others.

☐ Reading and studying the Bible will keep us centered and grounded.

☐ People will be attracted to the love of God when we extend loving arms of friendship and are enthusiastic about what we believe.

What I Learned

_____
_____
_____
_____
_____
_____
_____
_____
_____
_____
_____
_____

I'll Walk It Out By . . .

_____
_____
_____
_____
_____
_____
_____
_____
_____
_____
_____
_____
_____
_____

FIVE

I marveled at this man who was so incredibly nonjudgmental and who opened the Word of God in such a way that it touched my heart.

Kathy Golla

FORGIVENESS, MERCY, AND COMPASSIONATE CARING

I am the light of the world: he that followeth me shall not walk in darkness, but shall have the light of life.
John 8:12

She came to the Bent Tree Country Club, walked into the bar, looked around and thought: *It doesn't look like a Bible study is going to take place here. Did Donna really say the Bent Tree Country Club bar? No one looks "churchy", the place isn't "churchy", no rows of chairs.* Heads turned as this striking young redhead walked towards the bar. *I'll just lean against the bar,* she thought. Just then Donna Skell spied her. A warm embrace and words of welcome followed. Donna was beautiful—long dark hair, slim, attractively dressed—Kathy Golla admired her the first time they met. When Donna extended an invitation for Kathy to attend the Bent Tree Bible Study she readily accepted. Kathy had said, "I'm a baby Christian, and I need to learn more about what the Bible says." What Donna didn't know was that Kathy was very depressed, desperate for relief and was using alcohol daily as her primary way to cope. What Kathy left unsaid was that she had begun drinking in the mornings. She was an alcoholic.

That Sunday morning when Garry and Barbara Kinder were introduced to Kathy she remembers feeling very comfortable with them. "These were not 'churchy' people and I felt drawn to them. I was so young, only twenty at the time, but after those first few Sundays and getting to know them better, I knew he was a man of great character. I was drawn to that—to his leadership, the safety I felt in his presence, he wasn't threatening to me as a man, I knew he would never cross any boundaries. Coming to the Bent Tree Bible Study became a safe place for me to learn. There was no shame in not knowing scripture and all the Bible stories most people learn as children. Garry made it fun."

She had never known anyone quite like Garry Kinder before. She discovered that he had a strong personality. So did she. But, it was one of the things that she appreciated about him. "I have opinions," she explained, "and I'm not hesitant about expressing them. Sometimes he and I disagreed, but I must admit he was usually right." Her candor is refreshing. "Hopefully I have wisdom now," she laughs, "but back then, more than twenty years ago, I had a lot to learn and I was so vulnerable."

"As for Garry's wife, Barbara," she continued, "she was so petite and lovely. She had crystal blue eyes—like the water in the Virgin Islands or the Caribbean. She's the only person I've ever known whose eyes could smile for her when her face didn't. Her eyes were so welcoming. What was so amazing to me was Garry and Barbara's acceptance of me."

In reflecting about those early days of the study, she talked about the people with whom she was rubbing shoulders. "How was it that Mr. Insurance-man-of-the-world, Mr. Communicator-to-the-world, Mr. Sales, Mr. First Baptist Church of Dallas, Dr. Criswell's friend—all these titles, and I could come up with more, those monikers that can be attached to Garry—what was it that drew these people to that bar and to the Bible study so consistently week after week?"

She answers her own question: "It was God, and my spirit bore witness to that, just as the Bible says. *Whatever charisma he had, whatever spiritual gifts, they were God-directed, and so the people were attracted.* They came out of curiosity (a lot of them), and they continued to come.

"The people—how can I best describe them? Some were very affluent, others not at all. There were high-profile people, public personalities to shy and reserved individuals. All looked 'put together' but clearly seeking something. It was an incredibly diverse group. Garry helped create an environment of 'belonging' that was difficult to find in Dallas in general, much less in most churches. People flocked to hear Garry and share in the sense of 'belonging' without ever having to join.

"Coming from a 'worldly' background, I found my place at the Bible Study in the bar, too. It was quite a blend of personalities. We benefited tremendously from Garry's leadership and teaching. He became my mentor, my 'spiritual father,' and I sensed he was that to others as well."

But it didn't happen instantaneously. "Even after being saved my drinking worsened," she confesses. "I would drink before coming to the Bible study. I would sit in the back of the room feeling the numbing effect of the morning shot of Vodka. It had become more than a way to escape; it was an addiction. No peppermint made was strong enough to hide the fuel on my breath. But week after week I marveled at this man who was so nonjudgmental and who opened the Word of God in such a way that it spoke directly to me. I found myself wanting to be like Garry Kinder. I wanted to live the possibilities he talked about. I wanted to be a person of character and dignity just like Jesus. I'd hear him say, 'Study God's word, memorize verses from the Bible (hide them in your heart), and pray every day, specifically.' And in hearing that, I became convicted and convinced that I needed to face the secret controlling my life—chronic alcoholism and the pain and darkness that it sedated. I went to inpatient treatment in Arizona for eight weeks and then on to Kansas for an additional month of structured living in a halfway house for treatment of my drinking problem.

"Spending Thanksgiving and Christmas in treatment was a far cry from festive holidays in Dallas. I was in Salina, Kansas feeling very alone but sober. It was an odd place of miracles for those who sought them. There were street people living there and people who drank themselves there, like me. It was a State-funded facility for women. I didn't have a phone in my room, and I hadn't received any Christmas presents. I was freezing cold in that lonely room.

"There was a pay phone in the hallway downstairs and it rang. Somebody answered it and yelled my name. I thought, *'Who could possibly be calling me?'* I ran downstairs, picked up the phone and said, 'Hello,' and it was Garry Kinder. Of all the people I knew, it was this man who hung out with people like Dr. Criswell, Roger Staubach, Tom Landry, and others who were so well known—and he was calling because he was concerned, merciful and compassionate. He cared enough. He cared for somebody like me. *I was one of the reasons why Bent Tree Bible Study existed.* It was to reach out to people who had the potential to be somebody for Jesus. I will never forget standing by that pay phone that day, knowing that there was somebody somewhere who loved and cared about me.

"I said, 'Garry?' and he said, 'Barbara and I just wanted to call and say Merry Christmas and that we love you and the Bible Study is praying for you.'

"It's not just enough to hear about Jesus every Sunday; this man was Jesus to me that day.

"I came back to Dallas from Kansas, and worked with Anton and Donna. I was spiritually hurting. I was lonely and financially in ruins. I was a bankrupt woman.

"When I think about my relationship with Bent Tree Bible Study and Garry, I think about the biblical account of the woman at the well. I think about Jesus and how He went out of His way to go to Samaria to meet this woman in the middle of the day, the hottest time of day, the most uncomfortable, and she was there at the well. 'Tell me about yourself,' He said to her. And she did, and He said, 'Tell me about your husband.' And she said, 'I don't have a husband.' He responded, 'You're right. You've had five. As a matter of fact, the one you're living with now is not your husband.'

"I love that story. I see myself in that story, even though I wasn't married, never had been, and I was a chaste woman having made a vow to God to keep myself that way. But, there were a lot of people who abandoned me, and many of these people were Christians. Before I went into treatment for alcoholism, I was considered a fallen woman. I had this drinking problem. Most of us know someone who has fallen, in fact, we probably know a lot of people who have fallen. Many don't want to associate with somebody who has problems. And so the woman at the well was looked upon with scorn by the townspeople. But now she runs into the city and says, 'I met a man who knows everything about me and He loves me anyway. Is not this the Christ?' And the Bible confirms that the people came flocking to the well to see for themselves. Then they said, 'Now we believe . . . for we have heard Him ourselves, and know that this is indeed the Christ, the Savior of the world.' (See John 4:42.)

"Because of Garry's Christ-like influence, I was able to go on with my life. Garry put his stamp of approval upon somebody like me, coming from the other side, and he said, 'You can trust her. She has dignity. She'll work. She'll risk.' He believed in me."

Jesus made a new friend at an old well. The story of the woman at the well is an incredible account demonstrating the forgiveness, mercy and compassionate caring of Jesus. It happened!

Kathy's ability to relate to this account shows the relevance of the Gospel message for anyone today. Can Jesus use those who have failed in some area of their life in the past? Does past failure disqualify one for future usefulness? *Jesus had a new disciple, a new follower, and a woman at that!* There was a wonderful awakening in the Samaritan village because of her testimony.

Whenever God saves a soul, it is in order that the saved one may share God's great love and mercy with somebody else. If we have had our thirst satisfied by this Living Water, then Jesus would have us tell others.

The woman at the well came thirsty, but left satisfied. God's timing is so right. Jesus didn't demean her; He didn't frighten her off. In His actions toward her, we see tact, and the pure grace of God, the God who gives. Jesus treated this woman, considered to be at the bottom of the scrap heap of humanity, with as much consideration as He had shown to the respected Nicodemus. In spite of this woman's bad record and low reputation, Jesus chose her as the recipient of His second great lesson. When Jesus sent His disciples to the village (while He waited at the well), all they did was bring back some food; but Jesus saved a harlot, and she brought back the whole town! [1]

Kathy Golla says: "When I get to heaven and Jesus asks me, 'Now let's review, why are you here?' I'm going to say to Him, Because of three things:

☐ Bruce McKeever told me you were the Savior and I believed;
☐ You shed Your blood for me personally; and
☐ Garry Kinder believed what You did in me—what he saw and what he heard.

Jesus, that's why I'm here with You."

WHAT WE LEARNED

❐ Reach out to people in need.

❐ Encourage people in all situations.

❐ Keep pointing people to Jesus.

What I Learned

_____

_____

_____

_____

_____

_____

_____

_____

_____

_____

_____

I'll Walk It Out By . . .

_____

_____

_____

_____

_____

_____

_____

_____

_____

_____

_____

Part II

Courage to
Step Up and Step Out

SIX

I have often wished that I were a more devout man than I am. Nevertheless, amid the greatest difficulties of my administration, when I could not see any other resort, I would place my whole reliance on God, knowing that all would go well, and that He would decide for the right.

Abraham Lincoln

PRESSING ON

Forgetting those things which are behind, and reaching forth unto those things which are before, I press toward the mark for the prize of the high calling of God in Christ Jesus.
Philippians 3:13,14

"If we could get the Christian life down to where we should have it, it would really be an uncomplicated life," Dr. J. Vernon McGee used to say. He would point to these words written by the Apostle Paul in his Philippian letter and say, "Paul had whittled his life down to one point." Paul left the past behind with all its mistakes, unwilling to allow it to handicap him for the future. As to the future—Paul lived in the present in anticipation of the future. With that in mind he could write confidently about pressing toward the mark for the prize of the high calling of God in Christ Jesus.

That one point became important to Garry the more he matured in his walk with the Lord. He had moved his wife and two daughters from Detroit to Dallas in 1970, his career in the financial services industry was soaring upwards, and many things were claiming his attention. But one thing he would not neglect, or allow business opportunities and demands to do, and that was to crowd out doing what he could to advance the cause of Christ. To that end, having the interest that he and his brother Jack had in athletics, they both became involved in the outreach efforts of the Fellowship of Christian Athletes (FCA).

They met Bill Krisher, Dallas Regional Director, who was influential in FCA. It's one of the largest youth ministries in the nation reaching athletes and coaches nationwide, who in turn influence the youth across America. Garry was asked to join the Dallas board. In the ensuing years they saw the FCA grow dramatically in the Metroplex. Referring to the growth, Bill Krisher said at a "Champion for Christ" surprise event honoring Garry, "A lot of that was due to Garry Kinder—his commitment, long-range thinking, and his enthusiasm to see Christ presented to the youth throughout the Dallas area. Garry would do chapel services for the pro teams, for colleges and even speak in high school huddle groups. The thing I found exciting about Garry was that he was a man you could take in to visit with any pro team. They felt comfortable because he related to them with such ease about his relationship to Christ."

Bill continued, "Being a Champion for Christ, as he is, he's able to rub shoulders with many of the 'greats' across the country whom he knows because he's influenced their lives, even as they have influenced his in his enjoyment and appreciation of their athletic abilities.

"Garry is a dear friend, one of those men you could call on day or night, at any time, and he'd be there for you."

The Kinder brothers did a lot of things with FCA people, including two very special trips to Hawaii where they participated in seminars that included the greatly respected entrepreneur, Mary Crowley. Dr. Kenneth Cooper, Tom Landry, Roger Staubach, Fred Smith, Bill Glass and Richard Jackson were also in attendance. More than two hundred people flew from Dallas for the events. Today, the results of those events are still being felt in the lives of individuals.

"My brother and I were very involved in the baseball and football chapels nationally," Garry explains. "In fact, we helped start the baseball chapel, and we were involved in the early days of the NFL chapel with Bill Glass, All-Pro for the Cleveland Browns."

Garry was president of the Dallas chapter of the FCA for two years. "We met every month in Tom Landry's office. That's how I got to know Tom. Then we started doing chapel services, and I've done at least one chapel service every year since then for the Cowboys."

Garry recalls how he worked with John Weber, a Dallas Seminary graduate. Jack and Garry helped in getting him the position as Chaplain of the Cowboys and the Rangers, work he continues right through the present time. "One day I said to John that I needed a full-time minister to help with Bent Tree Bible Study. 'I need someone to do work that I know I'm not educated to do,' I told him. 'I can't marry or bury folks, or counsel with them; that's not my gift. I'm getting phone calls and counseling questions—ministerial type questions—and I'm not equipped to answer them. Also, I don't have the temperament,' I explained to John.

"John immediately picked up on this and said, 'I think I know the guy. His name is Rick Loy. Rick has two young boys. He goes around the country doing evangelistic work at different churches, but now that he has these sons, he wants to land somewhere so he can be there for them.' I was quick to pick up on that and told John, 'Boy, let me meet with this Rick and his wife.'"

That was in 1985. Out of that initial meeting and subsequent meetings with Rick and Jan Loy came a relationship that brought pastoral support, which had become so necessary for the Bent Tree Bible Study group. Rick explained that he was not cut out to be "the stereotypical church staff member," so this was a fit that was God-made for him.

Garry's humility and wisdom in recognizing that pastoring and counseling were not his gifts, but surrounding himself with people who are gifted in areas where he is not, clearly shows how God was directing in the Bent Tree Bible Study outreach. This left Garry free to pursue and use the gifts God had entrusted to him.

One of Garry Kinder's spiritual gifts is teaching the truths of the Bible. The Bible says that God has given each of us the ability to do certain things well. (See Matthew 25:15, Acts 11:29, and 1 Peter 4:11.) The emphasis is being a good steward of the gifts God has given you. *Use these gifts to help others grow in Christ — that way God will be glorified.*

Rick Loy's participation with Bent Tree Bible Study provided support and resource materials for Garry. "I teach periodically, provide the music for the Sunday morning class, and, because I am both licensed and ordained, I can perform marriages, funerals and baptisms. We believe in an outreach effort such as this, the leaders should function under the authority of the local church somewhere, so we are members of a nearby local church, just as Garry and his wife, Janet, are members of First Baptist Church, Dallas."

The Bent Tree Bible Study, therefore, has always had the endorsement of, approval and accountability to the local church for whatever is done in a ministerial role. "There's a real sobriety about the stewardship of this," Rick explains, "and it's not a 'hit and miss' kind of thing. Garry's commitment is exemplary, he is accountable and he is real circumspect about teaching theology. If he's not sure about something, he'll find someone who is."

I had noticed in the Bible Study that while teaching Garry would, from time to time, refer to Rick Loy for his opinions and comments. "Yes, he does," Loy stated. "It keeps me on my toes, believe me. I try to look at what he's going to be teaching on next, and anticipate, 'OK, what's he going to ask me on this one?' So it's been, and continues to be, a great relationship for us. We have all benefited from his mentoring, his leadership and his example of consistency. He never wavers. It is as fine a combination of business excellence and commitment to Christ as you'll ever see. The emphasis in the Bible Study is on biblical accuracy and life application—here's what we have learned, here's how to apply it."

Jan Loy related that when they first started it took them awhile to figure out what they were supposed to be doing. "Everything we had always done was very traditional, as in a Southern Baptist model of church ministry. So when we came here it was nothing like that at all—no membership, no system of formal accountability, no obligations. It was a pure Bible study effort, but I came to see the genius of it early on. I saw that it gave people no reason to make excuses—it's held in a ballroom in a country club; it's neutral territory. Come casual or come dressed up. You can be absolutely anonymous if you choose. You won't be asked questions about why you came. The format the Bent Tree Bible Study uses takes away all the excuses; it gets all of that other stuff out of their minds.

"To underscore what my husband said, the goal is to get them to listen to what the Book says. We show them that the Bible has relevance; it's timely, it's applicable to their lives. The study not only introduces them to the Scriptures, but to the person of Christ, and helps them realize their need for the Lord.

"Some people choose to move on from our class into a church. If they do, we can help them find a local Bible-believing church. We never try to become a substitute for a local church. We do pretty much one thing and seek, with God's help, to do it well. We systematically study the Bible and point people to Christ. We've never tried to grow a large group, but we see new people every year."

One of the areas of outreach that presented itself was the need for someone qualified to do counseling. Rick explained: "In the process of being involved in counseling people I realized that was not my strength. Yet the need was huge. And the need for trustworthy resources was huge. As the counseling responsibilities began to dominate my time, we decided we needed to find a professional resource person. But this person also had to be a bona fide Christian with a Christian worldview, with the best in methodologies and treatment approaches, yet all specifically compatible with Christian theology. It was about this same time that Kathy Golla came to Garry with the idea of starting a counseling center. We had met Kathy at the Bible Study. She was a recovering alcoholic, whose life had been dramatically changed, and Kathy was a counselor."

From this pressing need was born what is today the fifth largest non-resident psychiatric clinic in the Dallas/Ft. Worth Metroplex—The Bent Tree Counseling Center. The work of this ministry is told in chapter eight. How it came into being is illustrative of the way God moved in the hearts and lives of some of His children as they pressed for the mark of the high calling of God in Christ Jesus.

As one thinks about the Philippians 3:14 verse and pressing toward the mark, it is helpful to understand a little of the background that might have impressed itself on the Apostle Paul's thinking. The picture presented is that of a track star, running for a prize. Paul, no doubt, witnessed the Olympic Games—at least he had opportunity to do so since there was a great amphitheater in Ephesus, which seated one hundred thousand people. The Olympic Games were held there at times, and Paul lived in Ephesus for three years. In his writings you will find figures of speech that were taken from those athletic events. The prize isn't some earthly reward.[1]

Paul had received Christ into his life, and so he likens living life in the here and now as running a race so that he might receive the prize of eternal life through Christ. He knew that someday he would stand in the presence of Christ, as we all will. As Dr. McGee says, "I suggest that you get down on the racetrack and start living for Him. Paul encouraged the Philippian believers to get on that racetrack and press on for the prize—that high calling of God in Christ Jesus."

The Philippians verse is one of Garry Kinder's favorites. It is not difficult to understand why! It's what he's done with *his* life. Dr. McGee taught people to get down on the racetrack. The Bent Tree Bible Study encourages people to *step up and step out* for the cause of Christ.

There is no little formula for discovering the will of God. One cannot live a careless life and expect a vision or an angel or some green light to appear to show the way to go in a crisis. Knowing the will of God comes through a day-by-day walk with Him and a willingness to be led by Him. This will keep you on the right route through life, and it will be a great joy to your heart.

Dr. J. Vernon McGee[2]

WHAT WE LEARNED

❑ Nothing and no one should crowd out our commitment to the cause of Christ.

❑ When we trust God, He will bring the right people into our lives, as we press toward the mark for the prize.

❑ Life can be likened to a race, with the prize being getting to spend eternity in heaven with Jesus. We need to be on the racetrack, stepping up and stepping out.

What I Learned

_____

_____

_____

_____

_____

_____

_____

_____

_____

_____

_____

I'll Walk It Out By . . .

_____

_____

_____

_____

_____

_____

_____

_____

_____

_____

_____

_____

SEVEN

There was a woman at a well, one day
Near a city of Samaria, in a land far away,
There she met a Stranger, who changed her life that day,
For He gave her living water—from
The Way, the Truth, the Life.
She left her water pot, there by the well,
Ran into the city—for she must tell
That she had met the Messiah at the well!
Dale Evans Rogers, in *The Woman at the Well*[1]

GOING OVERBOARD FOR JESUS

Peter [came] out of the ship, [and] walked on the water, to go to
Jesus. But when he saw the wind boisterous, he was afraid; and
beginning to sink, he cried, saying, Lord, save me. And immediately
Jesus stretched forth His hand, and caught him, and said . . . O thou
of little faith, wherefore didst thou doubt?
Matthew 14:29-31

The account of Peter jumping overboard and walking on the water to get to Jesus is as dramatic a story as you will ever read. Dale Evans Rogers wrote about this with the depth of feeling that characterized her passion for what Jesus meant to her. Known for zeal in whatever she undertook, never doing anything halfheartedly, it came as no surprise to Roy Rogers, her husband, her mother, and family members that when she dedicated her heart and life to Jesus that she was, in her own words, "Ecstatic, wild with joy." Roy's response, as he looked at her with his penetrating, thoughtful eyes, was a cautionary word:

"I'm glad for you, Mama, if it makes you happy—and it sure seems to be doing something like that right now. But be careful, won't you? Please don't go . . ." and he hesitated before adding, "please don't go overboard."

She knew what he was thinking. Both Roy and her mother had her pegged right. "He didn't want me to jump too far, too quickly, too impulsively." Then she explained what "this business of going overboard for Christ" means. "The more I look over my whole great spiritual experience, the more I am convinced that the newcomer to Christ *has* to go overboard for Him. . . . once the vision of Christ came clear, I was like Peter—I wanted to go over-board—wanted to go the limit in faith."

Dale wrote: "Peter just couldn't help going overboard. He knew whom he had believed, and he was ready to lay down his life for his Master. . . . It can happen to us today, if we are will-ing to get out of the boat and if we want to see big things hap-pen for a big God. No, I don't mind folks saying I have gone overboard for Christ. He has done tremendous things for me; He has revealed great truth to me, and I will not let anyone laugh or threaten me into silence about that."[2]

When Kathy Golla returned from getting help with her addiction to alcohol, she knew she wanted to help others. How could she best do that? She worked and went to college evenings taking courses to prepare herself to be a counselor and work in the mental health profession. With the backing and support of Garry Kinder and Tom Landry, she went on staff at the Fellowship of Christian Athletes as an Addiction Counselor. "My passion was to help people with addictions of all kinds. Garry knew and believed that God had intervened and changed my life—he knew that God really did that, and so he trusted me. He went out on a limb, took a risk, jumped out of the safety of the boat, if you will, and stood alongside me. Garry believes in radical conversions; and he knows when they are not real."

Thus it was that she became the National Director of Substance Abuse for FCA, a position she held for four-and-a-half years. During this time, she was active in Bill Glass' Prison Ministry. He often invited her to accompany him and a team of people into the prisons. "I couldn't sing—others did that for him—

and I wasn't cut out to be an entertainer, but I could stand before those prisoners and tell them how Jesus saved and delivered me. I knew that 90 percent of people in prisons were there because of drug dependency—alcohol and other drugs—and once I saw how those prisoners related to what I was telling them, I knew I could step up to that challenge and step out for Christ."

She went into prisons across the country, often ministering to those on Death Row. Garry Kinder was behind her every step of the way. "He encouraged me. He shared not only through his teaching ministry at the Bent Tree Bible Study, but also through his lifestyle and the way he personally did ministry. He always said 'Yes.' To me he was the personification of Jesus. 'Go ahead, Kathy, do that. Sounds like a great idea.' I watched his life; he gave me permission to step out of the boat and walk on water."

Following her years at FCA, Kathy was recruited by a psychiatric hospital in a position for which she was uniquely qualified. Out of that experience came a burning desire to take what she'd learned about ministry at FCA and the good medical psychiatric health care she saw practiced at the hospital and blend them. Of course it was God preparing her and the way for the counseling needs that had to be met for Bent Tree Bible Study. She approached Garry and said, "I've heard you talk about counseling and wanting to reach more hurting people, and my heart just aches to do more and more of that. I would really like to do something like a counseling center. What do you think?"

His response was immediate: "Let me show you this office space right down the hall." And that's how the Bent Tree Counseling Center (BTCC) came into being. It's a remarkable story showing how God prepares the way and the individuals He has chosen to accomplish His will. We must always remember, God sees the big picture.

I think it's time that more Christians went overboard, got up and stepped out of their pitifully small denominational and cultural boats and got their feet wet in the great wide surging sea of struggling, suffering humanity. If we have experienced His love and forgiveness in our lives, if we have found healing in Him, if the Spirit has fallen upon us and empowered us, then let's speak up for Him; let's get going for Him. It isn't something we *might* do; it is an obligation.

I guarantee this: if you will keep your eyes on Him, He will never let you sink.[3]

Dale Evans Rogers

WHAT WE LEARNED

❑ Don't be afraid to go overboard for Jesus. If it is His will, He will empower you to attempt big things for Him—He is a big God.

❑ God can turn past error and guilt into present-day joy. The water He offers satisfies beyond measure.

❑ When we keep our eyes on Jesus, He will see us through.

What I Learned

_____
_____
_____
_____
_____
_____
_____
_____
_____
_____
_____
_____

I'll Walk It Out By . . .

_____
_____
_____
_____
_____
_____
_____
_____
_____
_____
_____
_____
_____

EIGHT

We are about bearing with one another, lifting up one another, encouraging one another. We are in the process of walking along-side people through the situations of life.

Smith Noland, M.S., LPC
Clinical Director, Bent Tree Counseling Center

BENT TREE COUNSELING CENTER: A PLACE OF HELP AND HOPE

Bear ye one another's burdens, and so fulfill the law of Christ.
Galatians 6:2

The Bent Tree Counseling Center Ministry

Rick and Jan Loy were on the founding Board of Directors of the counseling center, roles they fulfill to this day. "Kathy was the facilitator, the founding therapist and coordinator, and she brought on some extremely capable staff members. She personally interviewed everyone," Rick explains.

Today Bent Tree Counseling Center is the fifth largest non-resident psychiatric clinic in the Dallas area. On average, 450 clients are seen each month both as individuals and/or in group counseling sessions. Kathy Golla and Chip Dodd were the two principal therapists for many years.

In 1994 Smith Noland came on board to function as Clinical Director of the Bent Tree Counseling Center. After faithfully serving at the center for more than ten years, both Kathy Golla and Chip Dodd felt called to move on. They were deeply appreciated, their wise counsel greatly valued, and they have been missed.

Smith Noland, in explaining how the center functions, said: "We meet weekly as a staff for consultation, prayer with and for one another, and for our clients. We do active peer supervision and often work as a treatment team—not just as individual therapists sharing office space. It is not unusual for two or three staff members to be working with a particular family, helping the individual, then the family as a unit.

"Our mission statement defines who we are and what we do: *Our mission is to help individuals and families heal and grow in their relationships with God, with themselves and with others.*

"Our emphasis is on growth. Growth is a process. The way we go about the process is to literally walk alongside hurting people. We like to think of it in terms like the Apostle Paul used, the 'one another' phrases—bearing with one another, lifting up one another, encouraging one another, praying for one another. We believe that Christ is the ultimate resource for providing wisdom and directing our counsel. We don't always quote chapter and verse, but we apply biblical principles to every situation. We are always pointing the client towards the Lord.

"Each staff member has a personal relationship with the Lord Jesus Christ. We each depend on Him to be at work in our own lives and in using us to help others. We realize the special gifts God has given to each individual as members of the body of Christ. We respect and acknowledge these gifts in each other.

"Some clients in the midst of hurtful situations need special direction spiritually. Working alongside pastors and churches we help to provide what is needed during these times. Jan Loy, a member of our Board of Directors, is a real help in this area. Having been involved in ministry for over twenty-five years, she has a unique understanding of the spiritual process needed in counseling situations. Jan is on site to pray for or with clients as the need arises. She also helps with specific spiritual issues that surface in the situations of life. As we evaluate the emotional needs of each client, we also look for the spiritual areas of concern and try to help in those as well.

"The Bent Tree Counseling Center staff is equipped to work with most any age group or situation. There are therapists for adults, teenagers and children. There are a variety of "specialties" that range from play therapy for children, to individual and couples therapy. The areas of concern most frequently addressed are: depression, anxiety, marital and family conflict, problems in parenting or with children, addictions, and adjustment disorders. The center operates on a "sliding scale" based on the combined household income of the client. Private donations help facilitate this mode of operation thus enabling anyone with a need to be seen by a competent therapist.

"Bent Tree Counseling Center has become one of the largest resources for counseling in the Metroplex. The unique ministry started from the recognition of the need for counseling. Kathy Golla had the vision and experience. Then there was the committed group of believers from Bent Tree Bible Study who helped provide funding and prayer support."

Her eyes misting, Kathy Golla says, "It became a dream come true that was bigger than anything I could ever have imagined. There are children walking around who were to be aborted, but the counseling the women received at the center prevented that. There are drug addicts who prayed to receive Christ in Garry Kinder's office because we didn't have a large enough space for group therapy. Individuals who were depressed have received the help they needed and with that help they received hope. Marriages have been saved, families reunited. As for myself," she adds quietly, "I am like that woman at the well. Jesus went out of his way, stopped there, and conveyed to that woman 'I believe in you and I love you. Go and sin no more.' There are people all over — in prisons, patients we've seen through the years, young people, athletes, children — and when I stop and recall, I can see their faces, and I am humbled to have been allowed to share God's mercy with others."

This ministry continues to reach hundreds on a monthly basis — making a difference — offering help and hope and pointing people to the Lord.

Suffering is unavoidable. It comes without warning; it takes us by surprise. It can shatter or strengthen us. It can be the source of great bitterness or abounding joy. It can be a means by which our faith is destroyed. Or it can be the tool through which our faith is deepened. The outcome hinges not on the nature or source of our adversity, but on the character and spirit of our response.

Charles Stanley in *How to Handle Adversity*

WHAT WE LEARNED

☐ The Bible instructs believers to care, to encourage and to help one another through the situations of life.

☐ We should encourage others to grow and heal in relation- ship to God, themselves and others.

☐ Be diligent in prayer for those who need help and for those who provide it.

What I Learned

_____
_____
_____
_____
_____
_____
_____
_____
_____
_____

I'll Walk It Out By . . .

_____
_____
_____
_____
_____
_____
_____
_____
_____
_____
_____
_____

NINE

Regardless of the source of our pain, we must accept that God knows, God loves, and God is at work. We may not be responsible for what has happened to us, but we are responsible for our response to it. We must ask ourselves, "How can I walk through this pain? How can I benefit or profit spiritually from this?"

Charles Stanley in *The Blessings of Brokenness*[1]

A Tragedy Along the Way

...not as I will, but as thou wilt.
Matthew 26:39b

Jesus, while living here on earth, was living out God's divine plan for Him. He was human, yet divine. But in His humanness, as He faced the cross, praying in the garden of Gethsemane, he spoke to His disciples. He told them that His "soul was exceedingly sorrowful." Then He asked them to wait and watch while He went on a little further. He fell on His face, the Bible tells us, and prayed: "O my Father, if it be possible, let this cup pass from me: nevertheless not as I will, but as thou *wilt*" (Matthew 26:39).

When Jesus returned to where the disciples were supposed to be watching and waiting, He found them asleep. How this must have disappointed Him! His understanding of human nature showed itself when He said, ". . . the spirit indeed is willing, but the flesh *is* weak" (vs. 41b). Three times He left them to pray to the Father; and each time, upon His return, He found them asleep again.

If Garry had known what was facing him on October 31, 1990, and the tragedy that was to happen along the way, no doubt he would have fallen to his knees, crying out to God "Dear Father, this isn't what I want." More than likely, his next words would have been, "yet, not my will, but Your will be done." But sometimes when we are in the midst of the shock that tragedy brings, and then the pain of loss, the awareness of the sovereignty of God can be dim. It comes later when we look back and can gain a little clearer perspective. It is from that vantage point that Garry talked about the events that led up to and then the accident that claimed the life of his wife, Barbara, to whom he had been married thirty-four years.

"It was a beautiful Saturday afternoon in late October 1990 when Barbara picked me up at the airport. I had conducted a meeting in Chicago for a client company. We rushed home, changed clothes, and went over to Ray and Kit Smith's house for the celebration of the tenth year anniversary of Bent Tree Bible Study. Rick and Jan Loy had helped put the evening together.

"We celebrated the completion of studying the Bible all the way through for our first time. It was a happy occasion. I remember Dr. Criswell came out and joined us as a surprise. This was highly unusual for the pastor. His Saturday nights were very sacred as he prepared mentally and emotionally for all of the church services the next day at the downtown First Baptist Church. He gave such a gracious talk, and then the group presented us with a beautiful sculpture of the transfiguration of Jesus. Barbara and I talked about that gathering for the few days that preceded her sudden death. She loved that class — prayed for them, went to their ladies' Bible studies, and showed her love for them in so many ways. They, in turn, loved her dearly. Little did we know that four days later tragedy would strike.

"On October 31, my brother Jack, Donna Skell, and I, were in Orlando where we were doing a two-day workshop for Prudential Insurance. We had invited Donna because she made presentations about health [she and her husband were the owners of the Cosmopolitan Health and Fitness Center], while Jack and I talked about the professional, financial, personal and spiritual side of life at this seminar. My brother was speaking. I slipped away and called home — something I did every morning and evening. When I had called earlier, I couldn't get an answer. I began to get a little concerned and wondered if something was wrong because I knew that Barbara was to do a lecture that morning for Bible Study Fellowship. She was class administrator and a substitute teaching leader.

"When I couldn't reach Barbara at home, I called my office and my long-time assistant Dorothy James told me that something had happened; that Barbara was in an accident. Dorothy didn't have all the details yet, but knew that Barbara had been taken to the hospital. I got the number for the hospital and made a call. They put me through to the emergency room and the doctor answered the phone. 'This is Garry Kinder calling. I think my wife is there.' And he said to me, 'Let me ask you something— where are you?' I told him I was in Orlando, Florida. He said, 'Are you by yourself?' I said, 'Yes.' He responded, 'There's no one with you?' I answered, 'No. My brother's here with me. I have friends, but they're in the seminar. Why do you ask?' He said, 'Well, your wife didn't make it. She's dead.'"

Donna Skell remembers that it was 8:30 in the morning, Florida time. "Jack was in the front of the room talking. Garry came into the room and he was in shock. He came over to me and said, 'Barbara's dead.' That's all he could say. I was dumbfounded. I took him aside and said, 'Garry, let's pray.' It was a short , painful prayer. We motioned for Jack to come off the stage, told him, and immediately efforts were made to get a return flight back to Dallas."

Garry continues, "Barbara was out walking. She usually walked three-to-four miles every morning with two friends for her health. When I was home, I would jog the same route, and beat them back home because I jogged, and they walked. Since she had to lecture that morning, she'd told the friends, 'You keep going. I'm turning around and going back home. I have to get ready.' She got within three blocks of our home on Meandering Way and an SUV, early in the morning, not seeing her—she wasn't very tall— hit her when she stepped off the curb.

"Later, we pieced the incident together as best we could from the accounts of those who were there. When the two women who walked with her were coming back, they saw the accident. They were beside themselves, of course, because it was Barbara. They immediately ran to our house, but I wasn't there. So they went next door and got our next door neighbor, Greg Dodrill, who was in our Bible Study. His wife is a nurse and she ran over to Barbara. Greg called 911. The man who had hit her had stopped. It was certainly not a hit and run.

"A man in a jogging suit was attending to her. They all said he was cradling her in his arms. As the ambulance arrived, Greg's wife got in the ambulance with her. Barbara did not make it to the hospital, but was introduced to heaven at that time. The two women said they'd never seen the man in the jogging suit before or since. Later, I went up and down the street trying to find the man to thank him. No one fit his description. He was never found. Many of us believe that God had an angel there to take care of and comfort her in those last moments. Others believe he was a doctor who lived in the neighborhood. Either way, we do know that God provided comfort for Barbara in her final hour."

Greg immediately sent word to Rick and Jan Loy who, in turn, called the Kinder's daughters at their homes. Meanwhile, Rick and the Dodrills were waiting for the girls and their families when they arrived at the hospital. Karol Ladd, the youngest daughter, relates what happened:

"I was at home reading and preparing to teach a neighborhood Bible study, sitting in bed as it was early. I received the phone call from Jan saying that a car had hit Mother. In my mind I was thinking a broken leg or something, maybe a broken arm or ribs. My first thought was, 'oh, that's awful, she was supposed to teach the Bible Study Fellowship at Prestonwood this morning.' I immediately called the lady who was in charge of the teachers in the Dallas area and told her she would need to find another teacher. I then rushed my kids over to a friend's house. My husband Curt went on to the scene of the accident since we lived about five to seven minutes away.

"When I pulled up to the scene of the accident there was no sign of Curt. At the scene there were policemen redirecting traffic, but I saw no sign of family or friends. I could see blood on the ground, and asked the police where they had taken my mother. He told me they'd taken her down to Baylor Hospital. I protested, 'Baylor! That's so far away in rush-hour traffic. Why would they take her there?' He said, 'Well, Ma'am, that's where the trauma unit is.' That was my first inkling that something severe had happened. I just wasn't picturing it like that—how bad could it be walking along Meandering Way—it couldn't be that bad.

"I began driving in traffic. Driving and thinking—I can't drive down to Baylor Hospital by myself in this rush-hour traffic. I don't even know what direction Curt went; I don't know where he is. So I began praying: 'Lord, help me find Curt . . .' This was before car phones. I just kept on crying out to God, and then, sure enough, I looked ahead of me and in all that traffic I began to see a car that looked like his. 'Lord, please help me get up to that car, maybe it's him.' I never stopped praying. It was Curt. I honked and we both pulled over. I got in his car.

"I said to my husband, 'Curt, I don't understand why they took her to Baylor, but let's pray that God gets us there quickly so we can be with Mom.' I prayed that the doctors would be able to help her and that she wouldn't be too scared. Then I looked in the backseat of the car and there was a Bible. I immediately grabbed it and began looking for scriptures of comfort. I kept saying, 'Lord, give me scriptures to help us through this.' And that was the first of many miracles. I still am overwhelmed at this miracle to this day. As I kept looking for scriptures, I thought, *Psalms*. So I turned there. I thought, *Lord, give me comfort. Give me Your words of comfort.*

"Every scripture that my eyes fell on, every one of them talked about entering the gates of heaven. I couldn't find a scripture that didn't talk about heaven. It hit me that God was trying to tell me something as He wouldn't allow my eyes to fall on anything other than words that pointed to heaven. I turned to my husband and said, 'Curt, I think God is trying to tell me that Mother has died.' He responded, 'Karol, we've got to be open to that possibility.' I was shocked that he would even say that. I still couldn't picture on Meandering Way how somebody could die. It's such a 'no big deal' street—just crossing the street, how could that happen?

"I honestly knew God was preparing my heart and my mind for the possibility that she was in a better place. How loving God was to prepare me in that way—to give me His words: 'How glorious it is to enter the gates of heaven.' David, in the Psalms, often talked about how he longed for heaven and to be in God's presence. And those were the only scriptures that I could see. So as I walked in that hospital, I was lovingly prepared for the news we were about to receive. It was a devastating blow when Rick greeted us shaking his head, but somehow there was a cushion of God's Word holding me up."

Karen Smith, Garry's older daughter, recalls how they received word and responded. "We were at home in our little condo. I was pregnant. We were having our breakfast when the phone rang. David answered. It was a neighbor of my parents' telling us we needed to get over there. All he knew was that Mother had been in an accident. We weren't far from my parents' home on Meandering Way, so we quickly hopped in the car. I burst into tears: 'Lord, You can't let anything happen to my Mother.' I didn't want her to be hurt. But then, almost immediately, I knew that it might be really serious. When we got to the site and identified ourselves, the policeman waved us on. He couldn't give us much information, just that we needed to get to Baylor Hospital. By this time David and I were both in tears. We're driving down in rush-hour traffic all the way from North Dallas to Gaston Avenue where the hospital is located. I knew she was dead. I just knew. I was prepared.

"The amazing thing was that once we got to the hospital, Rick Loy was already there. That was so good—he was very close, like family. Rick is one of the most gentle, sympathetic men you will ever know. It was so good that he could tell us rather than a strange doctor in a little waiting room. My sister Karol and her husband showed up shortly after that. Rick stayed right with us.

"I made one phone call to my best friend whose mother happened to be my mother's best friend. Mrs. Byrd was in the Bible Study Fellowship class where my mother was supposed to teach that morning, so it was she who announced to the class what had happened. Of course they asked everyone to pray for the family, so by the time we got back to my parents' home, a dozen or more ladies were already there. Food was being brought in, and these women just took over, hugging and comforting us. Meanwhile, we talked to Dad on the phone and he told us they would be home as soon as they caught a flight. He was in a state of shock."

Karol remembers, "As the people started gathering at the house, it was a beautiful sight just to see them streaming in—these people who loved Mother. They were her close friends and people whose lives she had impacted. But one of the ladies was someone in the neighborhood that Mother would see every day as she went walking. She said, 'I need to tell you that as I walked by and saw what had happened, there was a man there who was holding your mother so tenderly. I have never seen such compassion and mercy in all my life as what this man showed towards your mother.' And remember, it was not a pretty sight due to the extent of her injuries. So it took someone with extreme mercy to be able to hold her, to stroke her face as she gave her last breath. God so lovingly placed this man there. Whether it was an angel or someone else—it was a man of mercy. And that has given us much comfort through the years.

"I also called the Bible Study Fellowship class to let them know what happened. The thought kept coming to me at that point about Elijah who, as he walked with God, was taken up, and I told it to her Bible Study Fellowship group. There was Mother, and she would often pray as she walked—not with her eyes closed—but she would walk and pray as she went. I think about how, as she left those two women with whom she'd been walking, that as she returned home, she was probably deep in conversation with God. My mother was a woman of prayer, a real prayer warrior. I could just picture her talking to God and there was a slight interruption, and then she finished the conversation with Him face to face. What a beautiful way to enter heaven!"

Karen recalls what happened when her father returned home in the afternoon: "Bill Glass and several others were there at the airport to meet him. When Dad came in the house, he hugged my sister and me, and then he went right back to the bedroom. Bill and I looked at each other, like 'What?' I remember seeing Bill, that big ol' man who always seemed to have everything so together, and I could tell that he, too, was just beside himself as he shared our shock and grief. When Dad came out he told us he wanted to see what Mother had been reading that morning. It was her daily devotional book, *My Utmost for His Highest*, by Oswald Chambers. She had her marker on the page where she'd been reading, and it was on faith and on the utterance of Job: 'Though he slay me, yet will I trust in him' (Job 13:15).

"He then called all of us, Karol and Curt, David and me, his two granddaughters, Grace and Joy, into the bedroom. He said we needed to be strong. Our mother was with Jesus. 'We will see her again. She will be waiting for us,' he said. Then he went to his knees and prayed. He thanked God for our mother's life. He prayed for strength for all of us."

Garry had learned about his wife's death in a very abrupt way. He was thankful for his brother and Donna Skell who, although they too were in shock, were strong support. By the time he returned home, and stepped off the plane, he was surrounded by more friends and his family. Rick Loy, Bill Glass, Gary Newell, John Keyes and Curt Ladd were there to meet him.

As loved ones gathered around Garry at his home, he was helped in the decision-making that always accompanies grief's work. Dr. W. A. Criswell, their beloved pastor came to the house that evening, sitting with Garry, his daughters, their husbands, and two little granddaughters, putting his arms around each of them, offering his love and consolation in his own incomparable way. As he sat there with Dr. Criswell, Garry couldn't help but remember that less than a week before, they had all been together for the happy celebration of Bent Tree Bible Study's tenth anniversary.

Garry recalls asking Dr. Criswell, "Do you think this is the work of the devil?" Dr. Criswell had responded by saying, "It was an evil act, but we should remember the words of Jesus, 'In the world you will have tribulation, but be of good cheer, I have overcome the world'." He was quoting from John 16:33.

"Dr. Criswell assured us that in this world there would always be tragedies. He reminded us of Genesis 50:20, the story of Joseph and his brothers who sold him into slavery. Joseph said to these brothers, 'You meant evil against me, but God meant it for good . . .' Later that week, at the memorial service for Barbara, Bill Glass spoke of this also." The memorial service was a true "Victory in Jesus" celebration with Bill Glass, Dr. Criswell and

Richard Jackson presiding.

Garry remembers what Bill had said at that service: "The devil means things for evil, but God will turn it into good." That was hard for Garry, his family, and all who loved Barbara to see on that day, but God did take that tragedy and turn it into good in many ways. Garry says, "Families were drawn closer together; marriages were strengthened; people came to Christ because of Barbara's death. Life is short; life is fragile. Barbara had so much to live for—she loved her two granddaughters, Grace Ann and Joy. She never did get to see her other three grandchildren—Lauren, Emily Ann, and Andrea—didn't get to hold them, play with them, lead them in their prayers, or to lavish love on them. Barbara was fifty-five. She had never been seriously sick a day in her life. She had the flu once when she was twenty-four. She was in the hospital to give birth to our two daughters. Other than that, she had never been sick. So for her to be taken this way was for all of us so totally unexpected."

The Bent Tree Counseling Center counsels hundreds of people who have gone through the grief process. In chapter ten you will read how they help people with their grieving.

> Faith, in the Bible, is faith in God against everything that contradicts Him—I will remain true to God's character whatever He may do. "Though He slay me, yet will I trust Him." This is the most sublime utterance of faith in the whole of the Bible.
>
> Oswald Chambers in *My Utmost for His Highest*[2]

Dr. Charles Stanley says that very often, when we are broken, we limit our perspective on brokenness to the physical or emotional realm. But the more important questions to ask in times of brokenness are these:

1. What is happening in the spiritual area of my life?

2. What might God be desiring to do in my relationship with Him?

3. How might God work in this time of brokenness to restore me, renew me, remake me, and remold my relationship with him?

4. How might God work in and through this situation or circumstance to bring me to greater wholeness?

WHAT WE LEARNED

☐ God's purpose is always accomplished ultimately at the
spiritual level. Outer circumstances may or may not vary.
They certainly change only according to God's timing.

☐ Our role in times of brokenness is to submit not only to
what God desires to do in our lives, but also to his
timetable. Wholeness may not come quickly or easily, but
it is worth the wait.

☐ When we find ourselves broken, we must be very careful
not to attempt to predetermine either the methodology or
the timetable for our own recovery. God will reveal his plan
and purpose to us step by step. Very rarely does He give
insight into the total plan He has for us. We are called to
trust him day by day by day.[3]

What I Learned

_____

_____

_____

_____

_____

_____

_____

_____

_____

_____

_____

I'll Walk It Out By . . .

_____

_____

_____

_____

_____

_____

_____

_____

_____

_____

_____

_____

_____

TEN

Grieving and loving are two sides of the same coin. A person who has never deeply grieved is a person who has never truly loved.

Author Unknown

GRIEVING AT YOUR OWN PACE

Let not your heart be troubled: ye believe in God, believe also in me. In my Father's house are many mansions: if it were not so, I would have told you. I go to prepare a place for you, I will come again, and receive you unto myself; that where I am, there ye may be also....
John 14:1-3

Dr. Criswell, in writing on these words from John's Gospel, explained that the word for "mansions" is found only here and means "abodes" or "permanent dwelling places." "Clearly Jesus knew that the disciples anticipated some such heavenly abode. He assures them that He would have corrected the notion if it were not true. The place where Christians will abide is a 'prepared' place. While it is impossible to determine its location, the believer is promised the escort of Jesus Himself, as well as eternal fellowship with the Lord."[1]

The apostle Paul wrote that love never gives up, never loses faith, is always hopeful, and endures. (See I Corinthians 13.) That was Garry's experience. Such is the way of love. The grieving process for each individual is different. "Some people get stuck and have trouble moving on," Garry explains. "I personally moved through the grieving process rather quickly." He quotes O.S. Hawkins who said, "People's lives are like a book, and there are different chapters. This is the end of one chapter.

"After you are finished with that chapter, you can read

and re-read it, but you need to go ahead and move into the next chapter." Garry didn't give up, he never lost his faith, he was always hopeful, he endured, and he was able to move into the next chapter of his life story.

Bent Tree Counseling Center: The Grieving Process

Smith Noland, from Bent Tree Counseling Center, explains the grieving process this way: "All people experience grief at some point in time in their lives. Grief is about dealing with loss. That may be a change in life circumstances, a change in relationship or position—or it could be the intense loss experienced in death. When any loss happens it can be very unsettling. Suddenly, the definition of things that are important to us has changed. A major loss—as in the death of a loved one, requires that we re-think, re-evaluate, and re-define what we are about and how we move into the future.

"There are five generally accepted stages of grieving:

- ❐ Denial—this can't be happening!
- ❐ Anger—directed towards self, God, others, or circumstances
- ❐ Bargaining—if only . . .
- ❐ Depression—deep sadness
- ❐ Acceptance—ability to come to terms with loss and move on

"These are not necessarily clear-cut stages; there is overlap and moving back and forth at times. There are no shortcuts in the grieving process. The time it takes for each stage varies according to the individual. The important thing to remember is that it is a *process* and that means moving *through* the grief, not trying to ignore it. It is also important to note that grief is not fully accomplished in isolation. We must learn to share our grief—with God and others. This allows us to draw on that strength that can only come from relationship and this prepares us to move on with our lives.

"As believers, we have an unwavering hope: we have something to look forward to; something better is coming! We have access to God's strength to see us through. We have the comfort of the Holy Spirit. We have the very presence of Christ in our lives to point the way. And we know that He has gone ahead to prepare our ultimate resting place. This knowledge brings us true joy today and great hope for tomorrow!"

Grieving Information That Helped Garry

Garry found enormous help and comfort through prayer, God's Word and the love and support of family and friends.

"There is nothing as powerful as prayer," Garry maintains. "When you are going through the grieving process you need to pray about it. You don't always know what to say, but you should just be honest before God and ask for His help. He knows what you need each step of the way."

Garry also found great comfort and assurance in God's Word. One scripture he found especially helpful was, "Precious in the sight of the Lord is the death of His saints" (Psalm 116:15). Knowing God's Word gave Garry the confidence he needed to move forward to the next chapter of his life.

Another source of strength was his family and friends. His family drew close and his friends surrounded him with compassion. Garry believes their support was a big part of his moving through the grief quickly. It was once again evidence of the truth of God's Word, especially when we act on it—*"bearing one another's burdens."*

The first Sunday after Barbara's death, Garry went to the Bible study. Barbara's absence was intensely painful, but there was also wonderful consolation in being able to share the grief. Everyone knew where Barbara was and everyone knew that the Lord would see Garry through this difficult time.

Garry's close-knit family immediately went into action doing the things family can do. They all learned to love each other even more. Garry's daughter Karen, and her husband David, were living nearby in a condo while looking for a home they could buy and call their own. "Mother got to help plan our wedding and she loved David. She saw her long years of prayer answered. My sister, Karol, was already married and had made Mother and Dad grandparents. They loved that. Mother was the best grandma! We had just announced in September at her birthday dinner that we were expecting. She was so excited! And then the next month, Mother was gone.

"After her death, Dad suggested that we move in with him while waiting to get into our new home. We turned a spare bedroom into a nursery. We kept each other company, and it helped us save more for the down payment on our house. Expecting the baby gave us all something special to look forward to—a brand new life while missing the one we lost. What a terrific God we have! It was a wonderful memory for all of us. We brought our firstborn, Lauren, home to his house. It brought him such joy. Dad was (and is) a wonderful grandpa! He plays with the grandchildren just like he used to play with Karol and me when we were little. The children love that!"

Garry recalls the day that David, Karen and little Lauren moved to their own home. "It was their last day living with me. Karen would always put Lauren in the baby swing in the kitchen as we ate breakfast. She would sit there and we would talk to her the whole time. On this particular day I said, 'Lauren, this is your last day here. You are going to be leaving me and going to your own home.' Right there in front of us big tears came to her eyes and she started crying. This was one of the most moving moments of my life. God had been with us and helped us and now it was time for them to move on." God is always taking care of His children—making provision to meet our current needs and future needs in ways we can't see at the time.

The family wondered how Garry would get along alone. Both Karen and Karol knew Garry needed to remarry. Karol talked about this: "Mother used to say, 'Boy, if I die first, Dad's going to need to remarry quickly!' This was something she said more than once and it was almost like preparation for us. I knew immediately that Mother was right. He was quite dependent on her for little things in life, as men are in so many ways. It was a reassurance to us to know that Dad would remarry fairly soon. It was okay—we were fine with that."

Garry recalls with gratitude that his daughters recovered "very quickly, remarkably well from the loss of their mother. We talked about it often, wondering how others go through loss if they don't have the assurance that their loved ones are at peace with Christ. We had peace and we had strength to work through the process of grief."

So it came as no surprise to Karen and Karol when, some months later, their father made it known that he was seeing a widow.

Even in his grief Garry had continued on with his work, golf, and teaching Bent Tree Bible Study. "Several months after the tragedy, Janet Hampton wrote me a letter saying she had known Barbara through Bible Study Fellowship. She said that she had lost her husband to cancer five years earlier. She also told me about some grief classes being held at local churches, and thought that maybe I would like to attend. Janet said that she knew what it was like to lose a spouse and that she would be happy to talk with me, if I ever wanted to discuss it. I thought about this for a while and then one day I called her. We arranged a breakfast meeting and quickly became good friends. Soon we began to see each other on a regular basis. God continued to see me through the grief and on to what He had planned for me."

"Weeping may endure for a night," the Psalmist wrote, "but joy comes in the morning" (Psalm 30:5).

A question often asked is "Why does God permit the righteous to suffer?" Many godly people have moments of perplexity . . . and from a despairing heart cry, "O, God why?"

The lesson we learn from (God's) silence is that He is never before His time, or after. He is always right on time. He is a "very present help in trouble." (See Psalm 46:1.) Although He seems to tarry, we must wait, for He will surely come. "Our God shall come, and shall not keep silence. . . ." (See Psalm 50:3.) His seeming silence is not one of callous indifference or helpless weakness, but one that is a pledge of the utmost spiritual good for the sufferer. With a glorious end in view, the Lord does not spare from pain, but makes us perfect through the suffering endured.

Dr. Herbert Lockyer in *Dark Threads the Weaver Needs*

Something to Remember:

The Divine Weaver

My life is but a weaving
Between my Lord and me;
I cannot choose the colours
He worketh steadily.
Oft times He weaveth sorrow
And I in foolish pride,
Forget that He seeth the upper,
And I the under side.
Not til the loom is silent
And the shuttles cease to fly,
Shall God unroll the canvas
And explain the reason why.
The dark threads are as needful
In the Weaver's skillful hand,
As the threads of gold and silver
In the pattern He has planned.

Grant Colfax Tullon

WHAT WE LEARNED

☐ People grieve differently and at their own pace.

☐ Heaven is real. It is a "prepared place" for those who believe in Christ.

☐ Faith in God, prayer, the truth of God's Word, the love of family and friends all help those who grieve.

What I Learned

_____
_____
_____
_____
_____
_____
_____
_____
_____
_____
_____
_____

I'll Walk It Out By . . .

_____
_____
_____
_____
_____
_____
_____
_____
_____
_____
_____
_____
_____

Eleven

Your love for one person will never diminish your love for another. Love never divides, it always multiplies. What this world needs is more love.

Dr. W. A. Criswell on the occasion of
Garry and Janet Kinder's marriage

GOD'S MULTIPLICATION

And we have known and believed the love
that God hath to us. God is love; and he that dwelleth in
love dwelleth in God, and God in him.
1 John 4:16

"The Christian life is a land of hills and valleys," said Scottish preacher George Morrison, basing his words on Deuteronomy 11:11. Solomon expressed the same idea when he wrote in Ecclesiastes 3:4 that "[there is] a time to weep, and a time to laugh."

Janet Hampton had experienced five-and-a-half years of widowhood at the time she met Garry. She had been married to her late husband, Harold, for over seventeen years. The last nine years of their marriage were spent in concern over Harold's Hodgkin's Disease.

"My husband, Harold, was a mind-over-matter type person, so he did fine. Nevertheless, the knowledge that he had cancer was always present. The chemotherapy was effective, however, about every four years he would have a recurrence. He would have chemotherapy again and be fine for a while. During the last treatment he experienced side effects from the chemotherapy that proved fatal. Even though we had been dealing with cancer for nine years, it was a shock when he died. We thought he would take the treatment and be fine as usual."

Although death is eventually a common experience for all, grief is a unique journey. Janet shares her journey: "Now that I have experienced grief firsthand, I have come to the conclusion that people grieve according to their personality. In a crisis, I am the type of person who takes care of what needs to be taken care of at the time. When Harold died, my focus of attention was on handling the funeral, caring for my children who were twelve and fourteen, and dealing with business concerns. When one has a physical injury it is usual to stop and take time to recover. With grief, there is a tendency to keep going. I certainly did. There was much to be done. When the crisis passed, it was only then that I took time to process what had happened. That is why it took me quite a while to travel through the grief process.

"After a few months, everyone thought I was moving on. In fact, the reality was just beginning to set in. After about nine months, I realized I needed to be around people who understood what grief is like. A friend told me about a six-week grief recovery class held at a local church. This proved to be extremely helpful.

"What was most helpful was an illustration that was given. Two circles were to be drawn on a paper. One circle represented me, the other, the one lost. We were told to overlap the circles to the degree that our two lives overlapped. Since Harold and I were not only married but we worked together most of the time, the two circles almost completely overlapped. The instructor said, 'Now, erase the overlapping part.' When I did that all that was left was a tiny crescent. This explained why I felt I had died.

"This illustration helped me realize why I was experiencing an identity crisis. My entire identity was wrapped up in Harold. Instead of saying that I was a bookkeeper, I would say 'I work with my husband.' When we went to church, it was Harold and Janet. This is what widows and widowers experience. Facing all of this is what the grieving process is all about. You have to start figuring all these things out and it is hard. It is harder for some than for others. Your body is using energy to heal your emotions. It is important to be good to one's self at this time.

"Another thing I learned was that when a death occurs, people are inundated with help from others and the church. It is helpful to wait about three to six months, then contact the person. This helps them realize someone is remembering. The illustration of the circles had been so helpful to me. After waiting until months after Barbara's death, I sent a letter with the illustration of the circles to Garry. Many people had sent cards and had written to him. I was just one among many, but what I wrote connected for him and he contacted me. We eventually met for breakfast."

Garry and Janet discovered they shared a common and deep level of spiritual commitment. Janet admired Garry's strong personality and his straightforwardness and honesty. She says, "He is just not going to lie; he just won't. I knew I could trust him.

"Garry and I realized we experienced grief differently. He always says, 'Everyone grieves differently.' I witnessed Garry handling grief according to his personality at the time his dad died. It was the same when his mother died a few years later. When they died, he cried very hard. He started dealing with the grief immediately. Garry went through the grief process quickly because he addressed it immediately. We have both come to the conclusion that everyone grieves differently. It is a unique journey."

Research shows that a widowed person who had a happy and fulfilling marriage the first time is more likely to desire another very satisfying relationship or marriage.[1]

After a few months of seeing each other, Garry invited his daughters and their husbands to meet him and Janet at a restaurant. Garry had already introduced Janet to his brother Jack and his wife Mary Sue. About two weeks later, Janet had the privilege of meeting his longtime friend since school days Gary Newell, and his wife Judy. Then there was a dinner party introducing Janet to Anton and Donna Skell and Rick and Jan Loy. Along the way, Janet also met Bill and Mavis Glass and Roger and Marianne Staubach. Everyone accepted her with open arms.

Later, Garry invited Janet to attend the Bent Tree Bible Study. Gary and Judy Newell escorted Janet to the study for the first time. The group accepted her graciously. Naturally, Janet started coming to the Bible Study on a regular basis and was later introduced as Garry's future wife.

Garry wanted his parents in Pekin, Illinois to meet Janet and in October 1991, he arranged for that meeting. Janet's parents lived in St. Louis and she wanted them to meet Garry, so that was done on the same trip.

New Beginnings

On March 4, 1992 Garry and Janet were married in a lovely private ceremony with their children and a few friends. In counseling with Garry and Janet before their marriage, Dr. Criswell said words that have come to mean a lot to them: *"Your love for one person will never diminish your love for another. Love never divides, love always multiplies, and what this world needs is more love."*

Janet was a discussion leader for Bible Study Fellowship and on the morning of the wedding she was there. Everyone asks her, "Oh, how could you do that?" She explains that she had everything ready and wasn't nervous. "The women fixed us a peanut butter and jelly sandwich for lunch. Garry picked me up in a limousine and we ate our sandwiches on the way to the church. After the ceremony came the fun part—Garry's sister-in-law, Mary Sue, had given us a cake to take along with us on the plane. We were in first class and told the flight attendants it was our wedding day. Enroute to San Marco Island, near Naples, Florida, they pulled out the cake, the Captain came on and congratulated us, and everyone was served. That was lots of fun!"

When they walked into their home, after returning from their honeymoon, Mary Sue had set everything up, Janet recalls. "She had stocked the refrigerator, completely cleaned the house, and even had fresh flowers for us. Garry had always been close to his brother Jack and he thought the world of Mary Sue. Now I was beginning to understand why."

One month later, they had a wedding reception on April 11. It was a beautiful occasion held at the Prestonwood Country Club ballroom (where the BTBS meets on Sunday mornings). The Bible study people were there to join in the celebration.

Garry's daughters and their husbands spoke, welcoming Janet and her two children into the family. Karol Ladd, one of Garry's daughters, said of their new stepmother, "We are thankful we can welcome Janet into our family as the woman who is making our father so happy."

Garry's parents were able to come down for that happy event, but in September of 1992 his father starting having stomach problems, which turned out to be pancreatic cancer. Following their marriage, Janet spent a lot of time with his parents in Pekin, caring for them. On February 13, 1993 Garry's dad died. Janet continued to go up twice a month to help her mother-in-law, but by June of 1994 it became evident that Garry's mother needed to be near her sons and their families in Dallas. She lived in a residential care facility for several years. When her health began failing, Garry and Janet moved her into their home where she could receive the care she needed. True to the nature of her personality, Janet assumed the role of caregiver. On January 12, 1996, Garry's mother died.

Dr. Warren Wiersbe, in his book *Be Obedient* relates how he was with the late evangelist Vance Havner at the Moody Bible Institute some years ago where they were each speaking. Havner's wife Sarah had an untimely death shortly before that. Dr. Wiersbe shared his condolences with Havner. "I'm sorry to hear you lost your wife," he said to him. Vance Havner smiled and replied, "Son, when you know where somebody is, *you haven't lost them.*"[2]

For the believer, to be "absent from the body" is to be "present with the Lord" (Philippians 1:21-23; 2 Corinthians 5:1-8). Garry and Janet Kinder and their family garnered strength, hope and comfort from those passages. They knew where Garry's parents were. "Blessed are the dead which die in the Lord . . . that they may rest from their labors; and their works do follow them" (Revelation 14:13).

God's multiplication continues. Garry says, "Janet and I have four children and six grandchildren. What a life we enjoy together! In marriage, I have been blessed twice — two wonderful women, both of them prayer warriors."

The love of God is one of the great realities of the universe, a pillar upon which the hope of the world rests. But it is a personal, intimate thing, too. God does not love populations, He loves people. He loves not masses, but men. He loves us all with a mighty love that has no beginning and can have no end.

In Christian experience there is a highly satisfying love content that distinguishes it from all other religions and elevates it to heights far beyond even the purest and noblest philosophy. This love content is more than a thing; it is God Himself in the midst of His Church singing over His people. True Christian joy is the heart's luminous response to the Lord's song of love.

A. W. Tozer in *The Knowledge of the Holy*[3]

WHAT WE LEARNED

❐ Your love for one person will never diminish your love for another.

❐ Love always multiplies, never divides.

❐ When we emerge from "the valley" we can continue to experience God's love and goodness for the rest of our days on earth.

What I Learned

_____
_____
_____
_____
_____
_____
_____
_____
_____
_____
_____
_____

I'll Walk It Out By . . .

_____
_____
_____
_____
_____
_____
_____
_____
_____
_____
_____
_____

TWELVE

The greatest thing anyone can do for God and man is to pray. It is the chief thing. The great people on earth today are the people who pray. I do not mean those who talk about prayer; nor those who say they believe in prayer; nor yet those who can explain about prayer; but I mean those people who take time to pray.

S.D. Gordon, *Quiet Talks on Prayer*[1]

THE PRIORITY OF PRAYER

Be careful for nothing; but in every thing by prayer and supplication with thanksgiving, let your requests be made known unto God. And the peace of God, which passes all understanding, shall keep your hearts and minds through Christ Jesus.
Philippians 4:6-7

Two very important questions are asked every Sunday morning in the Bent Tree Bible Study. The first is: What answers to prayer and praise reports do you have to share this morning? Every response given is a testimony to the goodness of God. Some are deeply moving, some have a more celebratory tone, but all remind the people that God is an attentive father, twenty-four hours a day, seven days a week. The class is reminded that there is always a long list of things for which to be grateful and offer praise:

❐ the breath of life that enabled them to awaken that morning;
❐ the health that allowed them to come to the class;
❐ the abundant food that was in the kitchen that morning;
❐ the choice of more than one thing to wear for the day;

❏ the shelter in which they slept;
❏ the transportation that brought them there;
❏ the friendship of other believers; and
❏ the unspeakable blessings of knowing Jesus Christ as Savior and Lord.

Add to all this the personal praise reports the class participants share and it becomes obvious that the thanksgiving should logically result in "thanks-living."

What prayer requests do you have this morning? That second, closely related question is asked shortly before the Bible study begins, and when it is, the group quickly turns its attention to the names and needs that are shared. Then, someone leads the group in a simple, honest prayer that God would attend to each of those individuals and circumstances as only He can do.

Praying, as you can tell, is a priority for the Bent Tree Bible Study. "Whether it's the formal group prayer time on Sunday, the volunteer prayer team, informal small groups during the week or individuals praying privately, one thing is certain, prayers will be offered regularly every week for every request. We take prayer requests seriously—both verbal and written," says Donna Skell. "*Garry often reminds us that Satan would have believers do anything but pray. Satan doesn't mind so much if we go to church, give our offerings or even read the Bible, just as long as we don't pray. Satan knows that God gets involved in a powerful way when His children pray.*"

God does get involved, and it's always encouraging to hear the weekly reports of how God answers these prayers. God's gracious responses not only give participants more reasons to honor God and thank Him for His lovingkindness, but they also build faith and trust that God really does hear—and care—when His people pray.

Rick Loy shared from his heart about one powerful example of God's heart being moved when His people prayed. Rick recalls, "One of the many answers to prayer the Bent Tree Bible Study has seen began during a retreat weekend. As a group gathered to learn more about prayer an expectant mom from the class was at the hospital to deliver her first child. The group received an emergency message from that mom, reporting that she had been informed by her physician that the soon-to-be born baby was in trouble, and would likely not survive after birth. The group stopped its study and began praying diligently for both mom and baby. That precious baby was born with some complications, and was a focus of intense prayer for many months."

Rick points out, "*Medically, the circumstance was never promising, but Heaven had a different view.* Today, Brittany May is an honor student. She is a remarkable, undeniable answer to those prayers. She's a terrific student of the Bible — a Bible Mensa student and knows it inside and out. She is a tremendous young person. So, it's been an immense blessing to the class to see a baby for whom they prayed grow up to be a normal, beautiful and gifted young woman. Brittany is a constant reminder that the last — and most important — word in any situation comes from God."

There have been hundreds of answers to prayer in the Bent Tree Bible Study — prayers for jobs, for those going into surgery, for those who were grieving, for those dealing with broken relationships, for people to come to know Christ personally, and so many more. They've seen all the challenges life presents, and every one of them has been an occasion to invite God into the middle of the situation. When the Bible promises that the effectual, fervent prayer of a righteous man availeth much, the Bent Tree Bible Study men and women would wholeheartedly agree. (See James 5:16.)

The Profound Simplicity of Prayer

The dynamics of prayer are simple enough for a child and yet deeper than the mind can comprehend. So, Garry and Bent Tree Bible Study try to help people tap into this incredible resource by providing lots of practical tips and user-friendly insights. Rick Loy shares just a few:

1. PRAYER — Prayer Releases All Your Eternal Resources

"The amazing reality of relationship with God through our Lord Jesus Christ is that we are actually members of God's family from the moment of personal commitment forward and forever. And, one of the most encouraging privileges of that relationship is that our Heavenly Father willingly and lovingly grants us access to all that He is, has and does. His resources are infinite; ours are finite. His perspective encompasses past, present and future; ours often struggles to see even this moment clearly. His wisdom is pure and perfect; ours is deeply flawed. His purposes are always just, right and for the accomplishment of His perfect plan; ours are colored by motives and impulses that may or may not honor God. So, the opportunity to benefit from His power should motivate individuals to make prayer a daily discipline of life.

"It becomes a very simple question: Are we living life out of our own resources, or out of His? Prayer really does release all the eternal resources of God in behalf of His children.

2. ACTS —Adoration, Confession, Thanksgiving, and Supplication

"How does a person go about offering prayer? Is one way better than others? Books, seminars, tapes, conferences and curriculum abound on the subject, but prayer is best learned via on-the-job training; if you want to learn to pray, just start praying. Nevertheless, there are some insights that may help you pray.

"**First, prayer is simply communication with God**, both *talking* to Him and *listening* to Him. So, set aside quality time in a quiet place to enter into this dialogue with your loving Father.

"**Second, approach God with the genuine respect and reverence He deserves.** This is a matter of your heart, demonstrating humility and gratitude for the privilege of approaching the matchless Creator of all that exists.

"**Third, organize your time with God.** The *ACTS* "formula" is an approach that our Bible study finds helpful. As you begin your time in prayer, spend time in adoration.

Adoration is simply praising God for who He is, acknowledging that He is awesome and holy. You'll find Psalm 66 to be a helpful example.

"Then, spend time in personal confession. This is being honest with God about your heart, thoughts, words and deeds, and asking God to cleanse you from anything that would keep you from enjoying full fellowship with Him. God hears every prayer, but the Bible makes it clear that He is most inclined towards those whose hearts are clean, open and honest. Psalm 32 and Psalm 51 can help you in these moments.

"The third part of the formula is thanksgiving, and it is just what it says. Spend time giving general thanks to God for the privileges of relationship to Him, and giving specific thanks to Him for all the expressions of His love and grace you have enjoyed on this day. There is no better example of thanksgiving than Psalm 103.

"Finally, supplication is simply asking God for His help, guidance and provision for people you know and for yourself. It's praying about anything and everything that concerns you. It's praying specifically—by name and detail—for the person or need. It's praying continuously, with an ongoing awareness of God's presence and sovereignty. It's praying genuinely, checking your motives and telling God the truth (He knows it anyway). It's praying confidently, remembering the truth of Hebrews 4:14-16. It's praying with a heart and posture of faith and trust. And, it's praying submissively, ready to accept the answer God gives just as Jesus did in the Garden of Gethsemane.

"The model prayer taught to us by our Lord Jesus Christ in Matthew 6 reflects all the components of the **ACTS** formula; let it help you as you pray. It may be organized in this or some other way, or it may be the spontaneous cry of your heart in a moment of praise or crisis, but in either case God waits upon you to pray.

3. PUSH—Pray Until Something Happens

"The Bible study has learned — as have believers through history — that the will and discipline to persist in prayer is often the defining characteristic of what we call powerful prayer. Starting to pray is one thing, continuing is another, but persisting until a definitive answer comes is an entirely different dimension. Luke 18 recounts the widow woman who, needing a just action from an unjust and uncaring judge, persisted in her petition until the judge responded in her favor. Jesus pointed out that if an unjust human judge could be persuaded by persistence, how much more would a loving father be sensitive to the cries of his children. Keep praying until God gives the answer.

4. Go, No, Slow, Grow

"God answers the prayers of His children — always! The answer may or may not be what we would design, but there will be an answer. Some years ago Donna Skell came across a clear and concise way to describe the possible answers God may give: Go, no, slow and grow.

"*Go* is a 'yes' from God to your request. And because God is a generous Father, that 'yes' sometimes goes beyond what you've asked and becomes 'exceedingly abundantly' more than you asked or thought.

"*No* is the answer no one wants, at least initially. But when it comes — as it does and will — it will be the loving and protective response of a Father who truly knows best. Every child has experienced the emotions of being told 'no' by a parent. And even though that child could not see it at the time, the parent responded with the best interests of the child in mind. How much more does God act in ways designed for our best? He seeks to make us more holy than happy, more wise than well, and more conformed to the image of Christ than comfortable. God's 'no' is a clear signal of His great love. The Apostle Paul knew this after praying three times for the thorn in his flesh to be removed. With Paul, trust His wisdom.

"*Slow* is another possible answer from God. He often uses the process of prayer to deepen a person's character, correct unhealthy behaviors or create a new understanding of spiritual matters. What seems 'slow' may actually be the quiet maneuvers of God's Spirit bringing you, others and His broader purposes together so that His perfect will can be accomplished. No one likes to wait, but learning to do so produces patience and renewed strength. And, what He does will always be worth the wait.

"*Grow* is a close relative of 'no' and 'slow.' In fact, it's a part of every answer God gives because He is always about the business of making us more than we could ever be on our own. Subordinating our wills to His is a growth process. Admitting our dependence upon Him is a major growth step. Surely trusting Him through the 'no's' and 'slow's' displays progress in spiritual matters. In the final analysis, every moment of every day is an opportunity to grow, and the process of prayer is no exception.

5. *FAITH*—Forsaking *All I* Trust *Him*

"This may be the clearest single statement anyone can make regarding the nature of prayer. Forsaking all means all human wisdom, resources, skills, explanations and options, including your own. Trusting God means believing that His intentions toward you are pure, right and positively purposeful, then thinking and acting in light of that belief. A spiritual framework built like this is an arena in which God may do great and mighty things. Hebrews 11:6 says that faith is necessary to pleasing God; that being true, faith is *the* essential ingredient in an exciting, vibrant prayer life."

Each Sunday when the Bible study comes to an end Garry prays with and for the group. He prays urgently and sincerely for each person present; for the families they represent, for the needs they are facing and for the grace of God to be at work in their lives. He prays for the senior citizens in the room as well as for the children. He prays for the married couples and for those who are single. He prays that the participants will have the courage and discipline to apply what they have learned from the Scripture in the just-completed lesson. He prays, and in doing so, sends the

> Your spiritual life will never exceed the quality and quantity of your time in prayer and Bible study.
>
> Source Unknown

group on its way with a strong reminder that prayer is a priority today and every day. It's an inescapable message.

WHAT WE LEARNED

❏ The best way to learn to pray is to start praying.

❏ If you want to make a difference, make prayer a priority.

❏ Prayer is honestly talking to God and receptively listening to Him as He speaks to you.

What I Learned

_____
_____
_____
_____
_____
_____
_____
_____
_____
_____
_____

I'll Walk It Out By . . .

_____
_____
_____
_____
_____
_____
_____
_____
_____
_____
_____
_____
_____

THIRTEEN

To most people (in twenty-first century America), someone who is "the salt of the earth" is someone who is a rather dull, plodding, conforming individual—a hard worker, maybe, and honest but pretty tame, a loyal churchman who seldom does anything outside of church.

However, the salt Jesus had in mind is stinging, biting, cleansing, and preserving and is anything but dull, anything but tame. To be the kind of salt Christ spoke about is to be on the cutting edge, in the fray, at the forefront of battle.

. . . (Jesus) did not say for us to become salt. He said we are salt. Once we accept Him into our lives we automatically are the salt of the earth.

Bob Briner in *Roaring Lambs*[1]

ROARING LAMBS—
FAITH THAT WORKS AT WORK

You are the salt of the earth. But if the salt loses its saltiness, how can it be salty again? It is no longer good for anything, except to be thrown out and trampled by men.
Matthew 5:13 NIV

Have you ever heard a lamb roar? Lambs bleat, right? Lions roar, correct? Of course! That's why, when I first saw the book *Roaring Lambs* by Bob Briner, I did a double take. I'm sure this title was intriguing to most booksellers and book lovers. I looked twice. The title grabbed our attention, didn't it? It did exactly what the publisher and author wanted. What in the world did Briner mean? What was he getting at? I couldn't wait to read the book. Talk about oxymoron—this was it! Or was it?

Time to Be Salty

It didn't take long to find out that Bob was right on—he was saying what many concerned Christians had been thinking. "Culturally, we [as the church and Christians] are lambs. Meek, lowly, easily dismissed cuddly creatures that are fun to watch but never a threat to the status quo."[2] We have by and large abdicated our role as salt and light in today's culture. It is time for us to be salty. Time to get out of the box. Time to stop preaching for just the choir. Time to be relevant—to show how the person of Christ *is relevant* to all of life in the here and now, to demonstrate to the watching world that we are for real. **Time to step up and step out.**

The Roaring Lambs book stated that every church and every Bible study should have a Roaring Lambs committee that meets regularly to discuss ways to be a force for good in your community and beyond. That's when Garry recognized the need and announced that the Bent Tree Bible Study was going to have a Roaring Lambs Committee. When he asked for volunteers, a great flock came together, bringing their own uniquely diverse gifts and talents and a common desire to serve the Lord Jesus Christ. One of those volunteers who led the way was Judy Bragg. Judy, along with many others, gave of her time and gifts to get this vital ministry up and running.

Soon it became apparent that a full-time executive director was needed. Garry relates, *"I mentioned this to my good friend Jim Dahlgren, and Jim said, 'The man for the job is John Gillespie. He's been praying about getting into some kind of ministry. I think he'll move to Dallas.'"*

The call was made to Springfield, Missouri, and plans were set in motion for John to join the leadership team as the Executive Director. John, and his wife Billie, brought with them almost twenty-five years of experience in the business world, as well as a heart full of desire to serve the Lord. Today, John provides the leadership for a new ministry called Roaring-Lambs.org.

Roaring-Lambs.org

John Gillespie says, "Roaring-Lambs is all about *Faith That Works At Work*. The vision of Garry Kinder and the commitment of the people of Bent Tree Bible Study to live life with a mind made up and a heart dedicated for service as unto the Lord, has made that the succinct and defining statement of Roaring-Lambs."

Asked to further define Roaring-Lambs.org John explained: "Don't curse the darkness; rather, go and be light. A Roaring Lamb is a believer who earns influence for Christ through personal excellence in the home, on the job and in the community. Roaring-Lambs.org encourages, equips and inspires Believers in this journey, helping them to be more effective in incorporating their Judeo-Christian values in their spheres of influence. God can use you to make a difference right now, right where you are and Roaring-Lambs.org is designed to support your consistent and effective witness in the marketplace."

Pray for the Nation

"They all joined together constantly in prayer . . ." (Acts 1:14 NIV). As you've seen, Bent Tree Bible Study is a praying class. It therefore stands to reason that prayer is at the heart of Roaring Lambs and the volunteer effort in the Dallas office. One of those volunteers is Janet Kinder who was inspired by 2 Chronicles 7:14, which calls for God's people to humble themselves and pray, so that God will forgive sin and heal the land. As she began to take these words to heart, the idea for "Pray for the Nation" was born. Janet says, "As those who love the Lord and our country, let us unite to seriously pray and fast for our nation, our leaders, and for spiritual renewal."

Psalm 33:12 says, "Blessed is the nation whose God is the Lord. . . ." Roaring Lambs encourages fellow believers all across America to commit to "Pray for the Nation," for fifteen minutes every Monday. They are asked to pray for a specific state each week. That includes praying by name for senators and representatives to the U.S. Congress from that state. Then it is suggested that they pray by name for a specific national leader. The state of the week and the leaders' names can be easily accessed through the www.roaring-lambs.org Web site.

The staff and volunteers of Roaring-Lambs.org point to the apostle Paul's words in 1 Timothy 2:1-5, "I urge then, first of all, that requests, prayers, intercession and thanksgiving be made for everyone — for kings and all those in authority, that we may live peaceful and quiet lives in all godliness and holiness. This is good, and pleases God our Savior, who wants all men to be saved and to come to knowledge of the truth. For there is one God and one mediator between God and men, the man Christ Jesus . . ."

Roaring Lambs provides a "Pray for the Nation" brochure, which is available upon request and contains scripture references to assist in praying for the leaders of our country.

Bible Studies in the Marketplace

Jesus prayed to God, "Sanctify them by the truth; your Word is truth" (John 17:17). The word sanctify means set apart. As God reveals Himself to believers through His Word we are led to set ourselves apart for a particular ministry. Many of the people of Bent Tree Bible Study have been inspired to lead Bible studies in their homes and at work, not just on Sunday, but every day of the week.

In January 2001, Roaring-Lambs.org began providing material for employee-led Bible studies in businesses across the country. The weekly Bible lessons present the Word of God in an easy to understand format and emphasize how to apply biblical truth in everyday life.

Steve and Laverne Bialas, long time attendees of Bent Tree Bible Study, are awesome examples of believers who thirst for truth from the Word of God. Inspired to live a "faith that works at work", Steve and Laverne host a weekly Roaring Lambs Bible study in their home and Steve leads two weekly Roaring Lambs Bible studies in the workplace. In speaking of this Steve explained, "Roaring Lambs Bible studies help to unite the Body of Christ in the workplace reaching beyond denominational boundaries so that people are encouraged. We have discovered that many people in the workplace don't know that the person next to them is a believer. By attending these workplace Bible studies, they identify with each other. People start sharing their joys and concerns, they pray for one another, and it makes a difference in their attitudes around our work environment."

John Gillespie said, "We are asked if an individual in the workplace wants to do this, do they have to get permission, and the answer is yes. We don't assist in this, but Roaring Lambs places a heavy reliance on the Holy Spirit to go ahead and clear the way. We do assist by providing via email the leader's guide, participants' guides and the necessary encouragement for a Bible study to be a long-term success. Our goal is to have every business in America studying the same lesson each week."

Roaring Lamb Seminars
"In the same way, let your light shine before men, that they may see your good deeds and praise your Father in heaven" (Matthew 5:16). John Gillespie says, "Because the majority of our waking hours are spent at work and at home, these areas of life provide a clear proving ground for our Christianity. We may have different occupations but all believers have the same vocation; we are ambassadors for Christ. A growing relationship to Christ cannot be segregated from any area of life.

"Garry Kinder had this in mind when he developed the first Roaring Lambs seminar, *How to Be a Roaring Lamb Leader*. Leadership makes the difference. This theme runs throughout this entire series of seminars. In the life of every person, there is a direct correlation between the quality of leadership the person receives and the person's ultimate performance. Jesus Christ is the best leader who ever lived and there is none better to emulate.

"Rick Loy challenges participants to honor God in and through our work. The seminar is, *How to Build Business Basics from the Bible*. This seminar is designed to help you learn how to apply your biblical commitments in the business environment. When you do so with professionalism and excellence, you earn credibility. When you have credibility, you have influence. With influence, you can be more effective in your vocation.

"Dallas business owner, Judy Bragg, has presented positive alternatives, teaching believers how to interweave their faith in all areas of daily life. *How to Be a Roaring Lamb* is a life-long journey of discovering and utilizing our God-given talents as a ministry in the secular community.

"Noted author/speaker, Karol Ladd, created *How to Be a Roaring Lamb Mother*, reminding us to never underestimate the influence a mother has on her children." Karol reminds us, "Not only are we the nurturer and caregiver of our precious charges, but we are also a participant in their training mentally, emotionally, and spiritually. As mothers, we have the ability to make a powerful impact on the next generation."

How to Be a Roaring Lamb Father, prepared by John Gillespie, calls for fathers to make a conscious decision to lead their families in the ways of the Lord. This seminar teaches fathers that leadership in the home begins with a commitment of faith and a willingness to stand firm for Christ, even when no one else is willing to do so.

Challenging—educational—inspirational—these are but a few words used to describe the impact Roaring Lambs seminars are having everywhere they are held.

Roaring Lamb "Hall of Fame"

Bob Briner often wrote and talked about individuals who had distinguished and were distinguishing themselves in the workplace as being examples of "Hall of Fame" honorees. These were people who weren't bleating lambs, they were roaring. "Hall of Fame" was a term he liked, but never sought this distinction personally. Bob Briner, right up to the time of his death in June of 1999, was still roaring, looking for ways to promote and encourage others.

The first awards banquet was held in December 1999. Garry Kinder presented the first award to Bob Briner; his widow Marty received the trophy for him. The second award went to Tom Landry, Jr. to honor his father Tom Landry, Sr. He was indeed a most appropriate honoree. He was a Roaring Lamb as coach of the Dallas Cowboys long before anyone knew what a Roaring Lamb was. The third inductee in that first year was Phil Glasgow — a man who stepped out and opened a Christian comedy club.

The second Hall of Fame induction was held in December 2000. The crowd was inspired by the testimonies of Roaring Lamb honorees, Charles E. Ragus, Founder, AdvoCare, and Norm Miller, Chairman, Interstate Batteries. Briner's words, "It's time for believers to confidently carry their faith with them into the marketplace so that our very culture feels the difference," were heard loudly and clearly.

The third annual Roaring Lambs banquet honored the late Mary Kay Ash, Founder and Chairman Emeritus of Mary Kay Ash, Inc., and Troy Dungan, Chief Weather Anchor, WFAA-TV Dallas. Both of these successful business leaders, through broad areas of influence, exemplified true faith in the Lord Jesus Christ. Dr. Jack Graham, pastor of the Prestonwood Baptist Church, spoke with moving eloquence of the need for Christians to get out of their comfort zones and be salt in the spotlight of public life.

In December 2002, the honorees are Lisa Beamer and her late husband, Todd. We'll forever be inspired to persevere by Todd's final words, "Let's Roll!" and the faith that has kept Lisa moving forward after that tragic day, September 11, 2001.

Where Do We Go from Here?

People wonder and ask, "Where does Roaring Lambs go from here?" John Gillespie answers that by pointing to the many people who have connected with and encouraged the leadership of those involved, all of whom are standing together to implement the vision that originated with Bob Briner. "Great people know two things," John points out. "They know how to get started to do a work that needs doing, and then they don't quit. And that's Garry Kinder. He knew how to get started; he had the vision. He imparted that vision to others who are staying true to the task set before us in order to make a difference. *It's faith that works at work!*"

To become involved with Roaring Lambs, you can do one of several things: Write for their brochure at Roaring-Lambs.org, 17110 Dallas Parkway, Suite 220, Dallas, TX 75248; call 972-380-1032 or FAX 972-250-3681. You can visit their Web site: www.Roaring-Lambs.org or E-mail: Lambs@Roaring-Lambs.org.

God wants me to study and obey His Word. I know He wants me to be salt. The Word tells me so. I want also to be a lamb that roars for Him in such a way that the sound becomes light, illuminating the Cross and directing men and women to the One who died there. He commands us all to do this. He gives us the privilege of doing this and to be in the arena, in the game—the one that counts for eternity.

Don't sit on the bench. Roar into action. Throw your head back, shake your mane, and really roar for Christ! The rewards are incalculable, beyond price.[3]

Bob Briner in *Roaring Lambs*

WHAT WE LEARNED

❑ You are the Salt of the earth . . . you are the Light of the world. Matthew 5:13-14

❑ Every church and Bible study needs a Roaring Lambs Committee.

❑ God will meet you right now, right where you are to help you make a difference.

What I Learned

_____

_____

_____

_____

_____

_____

_____

_____

_____

_____

_____

_____

I'll Walk It Out By . . .

_____

_____

_____

_____

_____

_____

_____

_____

_____

_____

_____

_____

_____

This is the house where Garry and Jack grew up. Garry was brought to this house when he was seven days old.

One of Garry's earliest birthday parties with Jack and their cousins.

Here's Garry at age one, with big brother Jack.

This is one of the most treasured pictures in their scrapbook showing Jack and Garry, with their mother and father, at a young age.

Jack and Garry having some fun!

Jack and Garry growing up, pictured with their mother and dad.

Garry in Jr. High playing his trombone.

Picture of Jack and Garry with their
mother, grandmother, and aunt.

Jack and Garry and their grandparents and aunts and uncles on their mother's side. Garry is the smallest boy in the picture; Jack is sitting over to his right.

The 5 young boys that won the 8th grade State Tournament. They went on to win the State Baseball Championship four years later.

Garry showing his left-handed swing.

Garry was a catcher and a left-hand hitter.

Jack, the coach and Garry, the captain, as they prepare for the national play-offs in the Junior Legion competition.

Garry and Jack, when Jack was coaching the team.

Junior League State Champions.

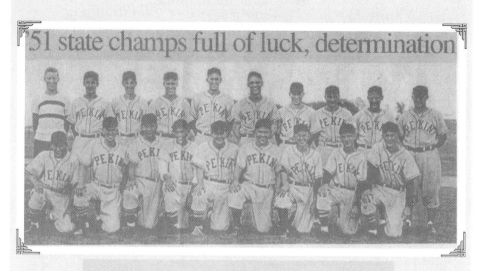

'51 state champs full of luck, determination

High School Baseball State Champions.

Garry, #24, at age 15, sophomore in high school, playing with a team that came in 5th in the State Tournament.

High school football team.

Garry's junior year of high school with his basketball team. Garry is #40.

Garry in his senior year in basketball. If you look closely, you can see his mother and dad sitting in the stands.

Garry's sr. year, #54. State of Illinois All-Star team from the south that beat the north by two touchdowns.

ILLINOIS WESLEYAN UNIVERSITY FOOTBALL TEAM
1951

Won 8   Lost 0

Undefeated, Untied, C.C.I. Champions

Back row L to R: COACH L. Bertagnolli, Trn. C. Andrews, R. Link, M. Smith, Capt. D. Clemens, C. Sharp, R. Bein, H. Bennett, C. Woodward, G. Melton, W. Keepper, J. Barnes, J. McLain, Mgr. B. McFadden.
Middle row L to R: C. Jensen, A. Giordano, D. Reed, R. Adomaitis, E. Deegan, W. Gross, J. Yohe, J. Chantos, E. Pierce, K. Sullivan, J. Tarter, J. Konvert.

Garry's undefeated college team. Garry is #67.

Garry and Jack the day Garry
graduated from college.

Attending a conference in Florida.

Jack, Garry, Mary Sue and Barbara
attending a conference in
Washington, D.C.

The great evening with Dr.
Criswell one week before
Barbara's tragic death.

Karen and Karol growing
up in Akron, Ohio.

Garry and Janet, pictured with Jack, Bill Glass, and Roger Staubach, with their wives.

Garry and Janet having a good time on a vacation.

Garry pictured with his good friend, Bill Glass.

Jack and Garry as young executives with Equitable.

Jack and Garry pictured with Roger when they wrote their book together, *Winning Strategies in Selling*.

Garry as a young executive.

Garry and Jack with two Hall of Famers, Carlton Fisk in baseball and Roger Staubach in football. This was in preparation for a baseball chapel for the Boston Red Sox.

Jack and Garry getting ready to do some jogging.

Jack and Garry with Olympic Champion, Frank Shorter.

Garry with Doug Sanders and Robert Stack, playing in a celebrity golf tournament at Colonial Country Club.

Garry with his two friends, Jim Moore and Jim Dahlgren, playing at Augusta.

Jack and Garry pictured with their mother, late in her life.

Rick Loy singing at a Bent Tree Bible Study.

Garry teaching at the Bible study.

Tom Landry receiving a plaque, pictured with Garry and Donna.

Garry, along with O.S. Hawkins and Phil Glasgow at an early Roaring Lambs banquet.

Part III

FOUNDATION FOR
STEPPING UP AND STEPPING OUT

FOURTEEN

It seems that we don't tell our friends often enough how they contribute to our lives . . . Thank you for being you. Thank you for being a treasured friend.

Sentiment from a friend, just one of many. These letters were part of a tribute book given to Garry during a 20th year celebration of Bent Tree Bible Study.

FAITH, FAMILY, FRIENDS

Praise the Lord! Blessed is the man who fears the Lord, who finds great delight in His commands...His righteousness endures forever . . . a righteous man will be remembered forever . . . his heart is steadfast, trusting in the Lord....
Psalm 112, selected verses

When the apostle Paul wrote to his friend, Philemon, he was, no doubt, addressing a man whose character and integrity were above reproach: "Your love has given me great joy and encouragement because you have refreshed the hearts of the saints" (Philemon 1:7 NIV). Similar sentiments and memorable scriptures were sent to Garry, placed in a tribute book inscribed **A CHAMPION FOR CHRIST: Garry D. Kinder,** and presented to him on the evening of February 2, 1996 at a tribute dinner in his honor.

"Loretta Littlejohn came up with the idea," Garry relates. "Loretta has been a faithful member of the Bible study for years. She has been a prayer partner and a financial partner. Loretta is a performer. Everything she does, she does well!"

It was a total surprise! It caught him off-guard and, in his typically unpretentious, almost boyish way, he was the personification of gratitude as he sought to find the right words to express his deeply felt emotions. "I've never been so surprised in my life," he said at the close of the evening's accolades. After describing how he tried to reach different people that afternoon, and being unsuccessful at it because they were all getting ready "to go to a banquet," he added, "There's a lot of places where you read that you shouldn't swell up when you hear things like I've heard tonight. But it's always good to hear them, even though you're not supposed to listen to them. But I do appreciate everybody . . ." and he reminisced about some of the people who had been a part of Bent Tree Bible Study from the outset, others who came later, and gratefully acknowledged all who contributed so much to his life through the years with their friendship.

Words at the Outset

Rick Loy, as emcee, said memorable words at the outset: "This is a surprise I know — long planned, much prayed for. We know that your favorite phrase at the end of your prayer every Sunday morning is to pray for the children and young people, that they would, in fact, grow up to be "Champions for Christ." And that phrase has made such an impression upon all our lives that we wanted to honor you and to say thank you for the life that you live before us."

"Precious, wonderful Christian teacher, beloved friend"

Dr. W. A. Criswell was asked to lead off with tributes. He called Garry "Sweet and precious, wonderful Christian teacher, and a beloved friend. . . . God did a wonderful thing for us in Dallas and for our dear church, and out here at Bent Tree Country Club when he sent Garry and his family down here to live in our midst. . . . You could find no more glorious example of lay leadership in the house and among the people of God, than my wonderful friend, Garry Kinder. . . ."

"No friends like old friends . . ."

Bill Glass spoke of the relationship he and Garry had as "One of the most long lasting and meaningful that I have ever enjoyed. There are no friends like old friends and our friendship goes back to 1963, and I consider you to be my best friend. I've had people make fun of me for saying that concerning another man, but I've also said to Garry, 'I love you.' And I'm not ashamed of that, because I don't know anything manlier than to be able to admit that you have a best friend and that you love your best friend. You were always there for me. I remember in 1964, we won the World's Championship, that was the year before the first Super Bowl, and you were there, praying and pulling for me. . . . Then when I retired in 1969, you were there, and we formed the Bill Glass Evangelistic Association.

"One of the things you suggested was that everybody write a check to get the association started . . . And where there's Garry, there's always [his brother] Jack. They served on our Executive Committee, Garry as Chairman for twenty years. He was part of the team and he was the quarterback. He got us started in the right direction. . . .

"Garry, I guess the reason you and I've always been so close is that we've always shared in crisis situations—crisis in pro football, in prison ministry, in citywide ministry, when Barbara died, when my first grandson was born with Down's Syndrome, when my son divorced, my recent stroke—always a crisis, we've shared in a lot of them and it drew us close to each other."

An Encourager Possessing Character, Integrity and Loyalty

Dr. O. S. Hawkins, at that time the pastor at First Baptist Church of Dallas, spoke with warm appreciation for the encouragement of Garry's friendship. "Hearing these testimonies tonight, I thank God for the attributes that you have in your life—character, integrity and loyalty. As I've been listening, if there's a common thread woven through the fabric of what we've been hearing tonight it's that Garry is an *encourager.*

"He's been one of the greatest encouragers to me. More times than not, I've opened the mail and there's a letter of encouragement, or a phone call, or a pat on the back. Affirmation is so vitally important in everything we do."

An Example — "One hundred percent straight arrow"

Gary Newell, longtime friend of Garry's, having known him since grade school days when they were in athletic events together, the friend charged with getting Garry and Janet to the dinner without Garry getting suspicious, spoke briefly but with deep feeling of their long-lasting relationship. "Some of the people in the audience asked me to divulge some things about Garry that nobody knows. In fact, they really prodded me. So that's one thing I'm going to do tonight — I'm going to tell you the truth — "I've known Garry for more than fifty years. I've never, ever, in my entire life, seen this man do anything, say anything, create any illusion with anybody, that you wouldn't have all been perfectly happy to have seen — not ever in my life, so help me. He is the example like you think he is — one hundred percent straight arrow — so I'm going to tell just one thing — I love you, man."

In his tribute letter to Garry, Newell commended him for the time and effort made each week in preparation and presentation for the Bible study. "As a 'Champion for Christ' you make the Bible come alive. You're an inspiration to us and many others the way you 'talk the talk and walk the walk.'"

Tremendous Courage, Friend and Mentor

Dorothy James Calhoun, who was Garry's executive assistant for twenty-seven years, spoke of those years with deep emotion: "Through all those years, I have never seen anything but a man with tremendous courage and integrity, unafraid to stand up for his beliefs.

"I've learned much from you and consider you a friend as well as a mentor."

A Contagious "Champion for Christ" Spirit

In that book, I shared these personal thoughts about Garry: "With much pride I tell people about my boss, Garry Kinder. I boast of all your many accomplishments and honors, both professionally and personally. I've seen you handle success and adversity with dignity, humility and wisdom — responses that come from a right relationship with God. It's good to be able to say to my friends and our clients that you are a genuine 'Champion for Christ.' I count it a privilege and honor to work for you. However, the most important influence you have had on my life, across the board, is always living like Christ before me and expecting the same from me. Thank you! Your 'Champion for Christ' spirit is contagious!"

An Example and Inspiration

Gregg Dodrill lived next door to Garry and Barbara for nineteen years and he calls Garry, "My hero!"

"The way you live your life has served as an example and an inspiration to myself and my family for nineteen years — an example of what a husband, father, businessman, and Christian should be. Our lives are much richer because of you."

Building Friendships

Bent Tree Bible Study has always stressed faith, family and friends. In times of trouble, this is what will sustain you. It's important to have close friends outside your own family.

Garry relates, "In the formative years, there were friends like Jack Bonjean and George Beres. In high school, there were people like Doyle Glass, Oscar Tharp, Les Plotner and Gary Newell.

"Gary Newell and I maintained our friendship through college, even double-dating on many occasions with Judy, who would become his wife. In 1970, they too moved to Dallas with their four daughters. We are close friends to this day.

"In college, I developed friendships with Jake Charvat, Al Meyer, Jim Stephens, Ron Bell and John Nottoli. They were all fraternity brothers as well as good friends.

"During the years in Bloomington, I had a neighbor by the name of Bob Gipson. He too was in the insurance business. He handled the property/casualty, and I handled the life. He was known in Bloomington as Mr. Insurance. During those years, I developed other close friendships with people like Jim Tague, Dick Ahlenius, Bob Scott, and Ken Miller. Ken and Diane are two of my closest friends yet today. They live in Phoenix, Arizona. They spent a lot of time with me following Barbara's death."

Ken has always maintained that the Bent Tree Bible Study had its early beginnings in Bloomington in the early 60's when the four of them formed a Bible study that met every Friday night. They would take turns leading the lesson. Ken says, "It was during this time that we developed handouts for each lesson. We kept track of hours spent every week in prayer, Bible reading, and witnessing."

Garry went on to say, "After moving to Dallas, we made many new friends. However, we continued to stay close to Ken and Diane who were living in Phoenix and Gary and Judy Newell who eventually moved to Dallas. Then in 1974, Jack and Mary Sue moved to Dallas and for the first time since childhood we were able to live in the same town, work for the same company, and accomplish the same goals. Kinder Brothers is now almost thirty years old.

"In the early days at Preston Trail Country Club, I played golf every Saturday with John Keys, Earl Summers, and Bill Frogue. In recent years, my Preston Trail days have been spent with Jim Dahlgren, Dale Dodson, Allan Duck, Denny McClain, Jim Moore, Phil Glasgow and Charlie Gaines, before his death. It is truly great to have friends that you can rely on in times of emergency.

"When we moved to Dallas in June of 1969, the first employee we hired was Dorothy James. She was one of the finest administrative employees we ever encountered. She worked with us at Equitable, and she was the first employee of Kinder Brothers. She was also the first retiree at Kinder Brothers. Dorothy attended Bent Tree Bible Study regularly, and still attends our Christmas parties. She was not only a business associate, but also a friend.

"First comes faith—faith in God; then comes family. The Bible tells us to take good care of our families. (See 1 Timothy 5:8.) And third, build strong friendships. **Faith—Family—Friends.**"

WHAT WE LEARNED

☐ Be an encourager. Give people a lift.

☐ Be a friend. "A man that hath friends must show himself friendly" (Proverbs 18:24).

☐ Be a "Champion for Christ." The apostle Paul wrote that we are to be an example to others in word, in conversation, in love, in spirit, in faith, and in purity. (See I Timothy 4:12.)

What I Learned

_____

_____

_____

_____

_____

_____

_____

_____

_____

I'll Walk It Out By . . .

_____

_____

_____

_____

_____

_____

_____

_____

_____

_____

_____

_____

_____

══ FIFTEEN ══

Adversity introduces us to ourselves.

President George W. Bush in his message to the congregation gathered at the
National Cathedral three days after the horrific events of September 11, 2001.

BUILDING CHARACTER

A good man out of the good treasure of his heart
brings forth good; and an evil man out of the evil treasure
of his heart brings forth evil. For out of the abundance
of the heart his mouth speaks.
Jesus speaking in Luke 6:45 NIV

Garry had learned from such men as Dr. O. S. Hawkins, Dr. Criswell, and Dr. Mac Brunson the importance of memorizing scripture. "They have said that many times we are not made in a crisis—we are *revealed* in a crisis. What comes out of us when the pressure is on is what we have put into our minds and souls. This is scriptural. In Luke 6:45 Jesus said 'out of the abundance of the heart [the] mouth speaketh.'"

Garry also refers to the influence of Sir Winston Churchill and Abraham Lincoln on his thinking. "They are my favorite people from secular history. I've read everything I can get my hands on about both of these men.

"Some called him 'Churchill the Magnificent' and for good reason. He was a soldier, war correspondent, master politician, orator, author, national leader, world statesman—in more than half a dozen roles, Winston Churchill left his mark on history. His finest hour, however, came as he led England through the dark days of World War II with dignity and exemplary fortitude and courage. If anyone knew how to face crisis times, it was Sir Winston. He was always in the heat of battle giving the V-for-victory salute and encouraging others. On becoming Prime Minister at the age of sixty-six, in May 1940, he spoke those memorable words: 'I have nothing to offer but blood, toil, tears, and sweat.' A month later, in the House of Commons, he proclaimed, 'We shall not fall or fail . . . we shall defend our island . . . we shall never surrender.'"

In speaking on the subject of building character Garry relates, "One of my favorite speeches of Churchill was the one he gave to his middle school late in life: 'Never, never, never, never, never, never, never in anything great or anything small, never give up!' That was the complete speech. That has really made an impression on me and influenced my own philosophy." Churchill was a dauntless leader who made survival heroic and victory attainable for his beleaguered people.

Garry points to Abraham Lincoln as another man who never gave up. It was a time of national crisis when Lincoln became President of the United States. Garry provides a review of Lincoln's life that clearly shows his tenacity, resolve and faith. "He was the son of a farmer and carpenter from Kentucky and one of four children. There was little opportunity for education other than what he himself acquired. He worked at odd jobs and as a clerk in a store. Later he studied law, and was admitted to the bar on March 31, 1837."

In his writing and speaking, Garry emphasizes that quitting is never an option. It is the determination of the leadership that keeps a company alive. "Quitting is a choice. It is not an inevitability, unless you give it the power to be one. An organization's attitude toward quitting begins at the top. The same can be said for individuals, families, communities, and entire nations." Then he provides the following list of events that all happened to just one person, and asks, "How would you respond if they happened to you?"

❒ His mother died when he was only nine years old.
❒ He failed at his first effort in business.
❒ He was defeated in his first attempt at running for legislative politics.

- ❏ He lost his job and could not get into law school.
- ❏ He declared bankruptcy and spent the next seventeen years of his life paying off the money he had borrowed from friends to start his business.
- ❏ He was defeated for legislature a second time.
- ❏ He was engaged to be married, but his fiancée died.
- ❏ Heartbroken from the loss of his fiancée, he suffered a nervous breakdown and spent the next six months in bed.
- ❏ He was defeated in another attempt at politics, this time running for state legislature.
- ❏ He was then defeated for the U.S. Congress; and still later, for the U.S. Senate.
- ❏ This persevering soul then was rejected for the job of U.S. Land Office in his home state; and was once again defeated for the U.S. Senate.
- ❏ Then he was defeated for Vice President of the U.S., receiving less than a hundred votes; and was defeated for the U.S. Senate a third time.
- ❏ Finally, this individual was elected President of the United States.

"Lincoln was fifty-one when elected President. His ascendancy to the highest office in our land came because of several very uncommon and unlikely events. The nation was sharply divided. The economy was collapsing. The political parties were badly splintered, so much so that the voting public had four choices to choose from for president, not the customary two candidates.

"It was with each of these unique events, all converging at the same point in history, that made the unlikely, likely—the election of a politically unproven outsider into the highest office of the land. The country was deeply stirred by the secession of seven states. One month after his election Virginia, Arkansas, North Carolina, and Tennessee also seceded.

"My favorite speech of Lincoln's was when he left Springfield, Illinois, and I'm paraphrasing, but it goes something like this. He was standing on the back of the train as he told the people that he loved Springfield because he was married there, he buried one child there, and he had many friends there. As the train got ready to pull out, he said, 'Trusting in Him who can stay here with you, go with me, and be everywhere for the good, I bid you an affectionate farewell.'

"You will find references to God throughout his messages. His first Inaugural Address was delivered on March 4, 1861. '. . . intelligence, patriotism, Christianity, and a firm reliance on Him who has never yet forsaken this favored land are still competent to adjust in the best way all our present difficulty.

"'. . . You have no oath registered in heaven to destroy the government, while I shall have the most solemn one to preserve, protect, and defend it.'

"During the dark days of the Civil War the president, in response to a resolution of the Senate, set apart April 30, 1863, as a day for national prayer. In his Day of Prayer Proclamation he called upon the nation to recognize 'their dependence upon the overruling power of God, to confess their sins and transgressions in humble sorrow, yet with assured hope, that genuine repentance will lead to mercy and pardon, and to recognize the sublime truth announced in the Holy Scriptures, and proven by all of history, that these nations only are blessed whose God is the Lord.'"

Lincoln's *Gettysburg Address*, delivered on November 19, 1863, at the dedication of the National Cemetery at Gettysburg is considered one of the immortal pieces of English literature. It seems fitting that at a time when our country is engaged in a titanic struggle to safeguard the very liberties that the brave men of Lincoln's day fought for, that we recall those words the President spoke: "Fourscore and seven years ago our fathers brought forth on this continent, a new nation, conceived in Liberty, and dedicated to the proposition that all men are created equal.

"In his second Inaugural Address, delivered on March 4, 1865, he acknowledged that neither party nor the North or the South expected for the war the magnitude or the duration that it had already attained. In plain words he stated, 'Both [sides] read the same Bible and pray to the same God, and each invokes His aid against the other. It may seem strange that any men should dare to ask a just God's assistance . . . but let us judge not, that we be not judged. The prayers of both could not be answered. That of neither has been answered fully. The Almighty has His own purposes.' He quoted Matthew 18:7, 'Woe unto the world because of offenses! For it must needs be that offenses come: but woe to that man by whom the offense cometh!'

"Then those immortal words followed, 'Fondly do we hope, fervently do we pray, that this mighty scourge of war may speedily pass away . . . with malice toward none, with charity for all, with firmness in the right as God gives us to see the right, let us strive on to finish the work we are in, to bind up the nation's wounds, to care for him who shall have borne the battle and for his widow and his orphan, to do all which may achieve and cherish a just and lasting peace among ourselves and with all nations'.

"Lincoln's life came to an abrupt end after the close of the Civil War by the bullet of an assassin on April 14, 1865, at Ford's Theater in Washington, D.C. He died on April 15.

"From studying the life of this great man, it can be seen that almost every time he was in a crisis, out would come verses he had memorized, the most famous being, 'If a house be divided against itself, that house cannot stand'. He was quoting from Mark 3:25."

Garry Kinder believes it's also important to memorize great thoughts and sayings from people of the past. For example, he points to this quote from President Theodore Roosevelt: "The credit belongs to the man who is actually in the arena, who strives valiantly; who knows the great enthusiasms, the great devotions and spends himself in a worthy cause; who, at best, knows the triumph of high achievements; and who, at worst, if he fails, at least fails while bearing greatly, so that his place shall never be with those cold and timid souls who know neither victory nor defeat."

In the weeks following the 9/11 attack on America, Garry read about Lisa Beamer's discovery of this quote by Roosevelt that her husband, Todd, kept in the bottom of his in-box. "The results of this philosophy manifested themselves in Todd

Beamer's actions and his last words while talking to the operator he had reached: 'Tell my wife I love her.' He then repeated with her The Lord's Prayer and said, 'Let's roll,' to the other men on that plane. Todd, you will recall, was on the hijacked United Flight 93 that crashed in the Pennsylvania countryside. It is believed that he was one of many heroes who led the charge against the terrorists who had as their target the nation's capital on that ill-fated day, September 11, 2001. It wasn't Todd's job to fight terrorists; he was just a passenger who, along with several others, did what he didn't have to do, but foiled terrible evil that might have been done to his country."

Garry has high admiration for Robert E. Lee and the integrity and character he showed. He often tells the story of how after the war when Lee was President of Washington College he would make it a practice of visiting the classes. "One day a professor was in front of the class talking about what poor character Grant had and how he was a hopeless drunk. Lee went to the front of the class and said, 'Students, today you have learned a valuable lesson. You never build yourself up by tearing other people down.' Then, turning to the professor, he said, 'Sir, as you know I am President of this college. If I ever hear you talk like that again, one of us will be missing from this college.'"

Garry values General Douglas MacArthur's devotion to duty, honor and country. He tells the story of when President Roosevelt went to visit MacArthur in the Pacific and sought to convince him to come home for a tour of the U.S. "This would have been politically advantageous to Roosevelt. He told MacArthur 'You should see all the changes—you wouldn't recognize everything there are so many new things.' When he was finished, MacArthur said, 'Mr. President, the things I believe in never change—duty, honor, and country.'" This was also the essence of MacArthur's last speech to the cadets at West Point when he did finally return.

The grass withereth, the flower fadeth, but the
word of our God shall stand forever.
Isaiah 40:8

In his Study Bible notes, Dr. Criswell explained:

This is a glorious affirmation of the total sufficiency and eternal existence of God's Word. Regardless of the decay of nature, human frailty, and changing circumstances, God's Word is sure. He gives absolute promises, which certainly will be accomplished. His word lives and breathes in the hearts of those who, through the ages, have been regenerated.[1]

In the New Testament, it is interesting to hear the apostle Peter quoting these very words from Isaiah. (See 1 Peter 1:24, 25.) "Peter stresses the enduring nature of the Word of the Lord. Flesh and all other materialistic features are destined for destruction. In none of these can one afford to place his trust. But what God says is permanent, enduring, and trustworthy.[2]

WHAT WE LEARNED

Garry Kinder learned many things from Dr. Criswell. These three are especially meaningful:

☐ The Bible is the inerrant Word of God.

☐ The Bible IS THE MESSAGE. One doesn't have a message without Scripture.

☐ Have the message so much in your heart that notes are not needed. Speak from the heart.

What I Learned

_____

_____

_____

_____

_____

_____

_____

_____

_____

_____

_____

_____

_____

I'll Walk It Out By . . .

_____

_____

_____

_____

_____

_____

_____

_____

_____

_____

_____

_____

_____

_____

Sixteen

The story is told of Major-General William Dean who was captured by the North Koreans. He was told he would be executed unless he revealed certain military secrets. He was allowed to write one letter to his son. The letter was to contain only one word. Major-General William Dean thought about this for hours: What could he write his son to get him past any roadblocks life had to offer? He finally wrote him the one-word letter—the word was integrity.

Source Unknown

DEVELOPING INTEGRITY

The integrity of the upright shall guide them.
Proverbs 11:3

"Absolute integrity is a delight to the Lord. Though men may be fooled and overlook an iniquity, God is present and is aware of every transaction." (See also Deuteronomy 25:13-15.)[1]

To live with the awareness that God sees and knows all and to have that as a guiding principle throughout one's life is to possess an inner peace.

Garry Kinder told the Bent Tree Bible Study class the story he had read in the newspaper about a waiter making minimum wages in a major city restaurant. "His wages were probably barely subsistence. He found a briefcase containing cash and negotiables in a parking lot and there was no owner in sight.

"No one saw the waiter find the briefcase and put it in his car in the wee hours of the morning. But, for the waiter, there was never any question about what to do. He took the briefcase home, opened it, and searched for the owner's identity. The next day he made a few phone calls, located the distressed owner, and returned the briefcase along with the $25,000 in cash that it contained.

"The surprising thing about this episode was the ridicule the waiter experienced at the hands of his friends and peers. For the next week or so he was called a variety of names — none of them complimentary — and laughed at. Why? All because he possessed a quality that is held in high regard — *integrity* — but, obviously, not by everybody. The dictionary meaning of the word explains: 1. *An unimpaired condition: SOUNDNESS. 2. Firm adherence to a code of esp. moral values: INCORRUPTIBILITY. And 3. The quality or state of being complete or undivided: COMPLETENESS.*

"A man of integrity is totally trustworthy. Solomon reminds us in Proverbs 11:1-8 that the upright person who has integrity of heart can expect three results:

1. His integrity shall guide him (verse 3). While others regulate their behavior by their interests and passions and the pattern of the world, he endeavors to know the will of God, and to comply with it in every instance. He will not deviate from this rule, even when it leads in direct opposition to his dearest interests and friendships.

2. His integrity shall keep him (verse 4). There will be wandering up side streets; even traveling up a few blind alleys, maybe for a time chasing down a dream, let's say, on Hollywood Blvd., but a man's integrity, his righteousness, will rectify his way. The man of integrity cannot enjoy pleasure in the way of self or sin. It is contrary to the tastes that have been developed through a lifetime of seeking to live in accord with what God says. God will preserve the ways of a man or woman determined to be a person of integrity.

3. His integrity will deliver him (verse 6). That is his safety net in the time of trouble. This is his peace during the time of fear and anxiety. Psalm 25 declares 'Let integrity and uprightness preserve me; for I wait on Thee'. That is not misplaced dependence. God can be trusted to keep His

Word. Psalm 26 goes on to say, 'Judge me, O LORD; for I have walked in mine integrity: I have trusted also in the LORD; *therefore* I shall not slide' (vs. 1). That entire Psalm speaks of the value of being a person of integrity in contrast to evildoers and those who prefer wickedness. When the Psalmist comes to the end of his dissertation he says, 'But as for me, I will walk in mine integrity: redeem me, and be merciful unto me. My foot standeth in an even place...' (vs. 11, 12).

" 'A person's faith needs to be backed up by a good life,' Dr. J. Vernon McGee wrote. Even though this Psalm was written by David who had committed a great sin, David didn't continue to live in that sin. It was because of his faith in the Lord that David didn't slide, that he could say 'My foot standeth in an even place.' Not that he was so strong, McGee said, David knew he wasn't, but he knew that when he trusted the Lord, the Lord would sustain him. David was surefooted, established on the Rock. When you are on a slippery slope, you are apt to fall. A lot of Christians are in that position today. Warren W. Wiersbe (*The Integrity Crisis*) says these are serious days for the church, that there is an integrity crisis, and let us not forget that the 'church' is us. We are it to the watching world.

"Wiersbe underscores something we should all know— there is no place for 'deceit' in the ministry of the gospel and in the life of that one who calls himself a Christian. Fraud and faith just don't go together. To fall for that which is fraudulent indicates a lack of spiritual discernment. 'What we believe determines how we behave, and both determine what we will become. If we believe the truth, the truth will sanctify us (See John 17:17.) and set us free. (See John 8:31-32.) If we believe lies, we will gradually *become a lie* as we lose our integrity and begin to practice duplicity.'"[2]

It is said that if you want to learn what a person is really like, ask three questions:

❐ What makes him laugh?
❐ What really makes him angry?
❐ What makes him weep?

"What we need today is not anger but *anguish . . .The difference between anger and anguish is a broken heart.*"³ What usually follows anguish and a broken heart is weeping. The condition of the world today should arouse anguish and weeping; a crying out to God to help us preserve our integrity as we interface with those whom we come in contact. There is so much compromise. Values we hold dear are constantly held up to ridicule by much of the media. How much we need to be intercessors. We need to be willing to take a stand for that which is right. Oswald Chambers wrote that God never gives us discernment in order that we may criticize, but that we may intercede. God's people should be *pray-ers*. To be intercessors, we must be willing to face facts honestly and not be soft on sin. This calls for us to be men and women of integrity.

Jesus left us here to be His witnesses to tell people how to be saved. Jesus isn't building a Mutual Admiration Society; He's building His Church.

Warren W. Wiersbe in *The Integrity Crisis*⁴

WHAT WE LEARNED

☐ We are to be people of integrity who know the difference between right and wrong.

☐ God will hold each of us responsible for the way we live. Integrity is a delight to the Lord.

☐ Proverbs has much to say about integrity. Proverbs 11:3 is a watchword for each of us: "The integrity of the upright shall guide them."

What I Learned

_____
_____
_____
_____
_____
_____
_____
_____
_____
_____
_____
_____

I'll Walk It Out By . . .

_____
_____
_____
_____
_____
_____
_____
_____
_____
_____
_____
_____
_____
_____
_____
_____

═══ SEVENTEEN ═══

It is better to die for something than to live for nothing.

Dr. Bob Jones, Sr.

STEP UP AND STEP OUT

*Wherefore seeing we also are compassed about with so great
a cloud of witnesses, let us lay aside every weight, and the sin
which doth so easily beset us, and let us run with patience
the race that is set before us.*
Hebrews 12:1

On many occasions during the Bible study, Garry speaks about stepping up and stepping out. It's a theme repeated quite often in the first few verses of the Old Testament book of Joshua. This book is actually a book of conflict and conquest and presents important principles for Believers to apply in their lives today. In fact, the New Testament counterpart to the book of Joshua is the book of Ephesians. There the apostle Paul expounds on Believers' position in Christ and what their corresponding responsibilities should be in Christian living.

The parallel between these two books of the Bible is most interesting. The apostle Paul emphasized that the Believer is blessed with all spiritual blessings, but the practical possession and experience of them depended upon conflict and conquest. Did these early Christians get it? "The cloud of witnesses" that the book of Hebrews talks about (mentioned at the outset of this chapter) bears powerful testimony to the indisputable fact that yes, they got it; many of them paid for it with their very lives. The blood of the early Christians as martyrs for the sake of remaining true to what they had learned about Christ, confirms their obedience as they stepped into conflict and conquest.

As for Joshua, he was the successor of Moses, divinely commissioned by God to take the people of Israel into the Promised Land. How would you have liked to step into the shoes of Moses? The conquest of Canaan was a formidable assignment. But at the outset, as God instructed Joshua to lead the people over the Jordan, He promised that if Joshua would obey and step up and step out, he and the people would succeed in their conquest. To read what God promised Joshua is to recognize that what Joshua did provides a pattern by which Believers in any age can possess what God wants to give them. Here's what God instructed Joshua to do:

> Every place that the sole of your foot shall tread upon, that have I given unto you, as I said unto Moses. . . . There shall not any man be able to stand before thee all the days of thy life: as I was with Moses, so I will be with thee: I will not fail thee, nor forsake thee. Be strong and of good courage: for unto this people shalt thou divide for an inheritance the land, which I sware unto their fathers to give them. Only be thou strong and very courageous, that thou mayest observe to do according to all the law, which Moses my servant commanded thee: turn not from it to the right hand or to the left, that thou mayest prosper whithersoever thou goest. This book of the law shall not depart out of thy mouth; but thou shalt meditate therein day and night, that thou mayest observe to do according to all that is written therein: for then thou shalt make thy way prosperous, and then thou shalt have good success. Have not I commanded thee? Be strong and of good courage; be not afraid, neither be thou dismayed: for the LORD thy God is with thee whithersoever thou goest.
>
> Joshua 1: 3-9

Time and Hard Work

Garry reminds the class that stepping up and stepping out takes time and hard work and you can also expect some degree of criticism. He quotes Thomas Edison who said, "Opportunity is wasted by most people because it is dressed in overalls and looks like work." The only way to avoid criticism is to do nothing and be nothing. John Mason has said, "A Christian is not called to respond to the critic. He is called to respond to God."

The word "work" appears in the Bible 564 times. Unafraid of work, those who had committed themselves to working with the Bent Tree Bible Study, became involved in a number of ways—some of which have already been told in this book. The following are other examples of how Bent Tree Bible Study has reached out to others.

The Women's Bible Study

The women's weekly Bible study was "a little outreach that was formed early on," as Donna Skell recalls. It's been in existence for more than twenty years. They've always met at the home of one of their faithful BTBS attendees. Connie Tolbert is one of those whose gift of hospitality has prompted her to open up her home. "It's a small group—usually twenty women — and we meet to share prayer requests and study the Bible. Jan Loy leads the study," Donna explains. "She's the most gifted women's Bible study leader I've ever known. Jan also teaches a Bible study in a high-rise condo every Thursday morning. She is a living example of stepping up and stepping out." One could call her a female version of Joshua. Her obedience is exemplary. Jan's love for the Lord shines through; it draws others to Him.

Donna says, "Some of these women have been in the group since the beginning; others have come and gone. One thing remains constant: God continues to draw women to this group who do not know Him and transform their lives by the power of His Word. They come, they listen, they share and eventually, they become Believers. Many of them have moved on and share their faith with others."

Jan knows who she is as God's servant and continually submits herself to His will. Jan says, "When we keep ourselves yielded to the Holy Spirit, he continues to order our steps and give us opportunities to reach out to others." And that's just what these women continue to do.

The BTBS Breakfast Outreaches

There is a quarterly Sunday morning breakfast outreach that brings people who may not attend the class regularly. Garry speaks of these breakfasts with a great deal of enthusiasm. "We send invitations and use this as an opportunity to bring others, usually unchurched friends. They are always well attended. We have them about three or four times a year, and feature a well-known athlete or someone with name recognition from the Christian world. We've had Roger Staubach, Tom Landry, Grant Teaff, O. S. Hawkins, Richard Jackson, Bill Glass, Jack Kinder, Jack Graham, Dr. W. A. Criswell and many others as guest speakers at these breakfasts. We begin with a breakfast buffet followed by special music, after which the guest speaks." Garry always gives an abbreviated lesson as a sample of what to expect on a regular basis.

The Bill Glass Ministry

Garry explains, "We've had Bill Glass speak many times. Bill and I go back a long way. We met initially in 1963 when he was playing football for the Cleveland Browns. He'd been traded from Detroit to Cleveland. I was building an insurance agency in Akron, Ohio at the time. We became very good friends. My wife and I, along with our two daughters who were just toddlers, attended every game with Bill's wife, Mavis, and their children who were also just little kids.

"Bill's story has always held the interest of our Bible study. It is an amazing story, another example of someone who stepped up and stepped out. Here was a man sold out to Christ—he was playing pro football, finishing seminary training, starting the evangelistic association, and he was a young father. Today he has the most effective prison ministry in history."

In speaking of the long friendship he and Garry have enjoyed, Bill recalled how Garry would phone him before every game. "He'd tell me, 'I'm praying for you. . . .' He would inspire and motivate me to play my very best so I could give the glory to God. We developed a very close relationship during those years I was with the Browns." It is understandable why he asked Garry to become Chairman of the Board of Directors for the Bill Glass Evangelistic Association.

"Garry was our Board chairman for twenty years — he's been by far the longest serving chairman of the Board that we've ever had. Now he's Vice-Chairman."

Back to Joshua

Take some time to go back and read the book of Joshua. Think about how God formed the nation of Israel in the brickyards of Egypt. That was backbreaking, hard work! Think about how they wandered in the desert for forty years after Moses led them out of Egypt. The book of Joshua completes the redemption of Israel that was begun in Exodus. Exodus is the book of redemption *out* of Egypt; Joshua is the book of redemption *into* the Promised Land. But the people needed a leader and God had prepared just such a man.

The book of Joshua tells us how to lay claim to the spiritual blessings that are ours through our Savior, our "Joshua." Spiritual blessings come as we obey God's Word, stand strong, and are of good courage. Joshua was told to not be afraid or dismayed, because God would be with him. Joshua took charge, and he didn't do it by being presumptuous, but in confidence believing God, because God told him what had to be done.

The Bent Tree Bible Study has been blessed as their Bible study leader has encouraged them to follow Joshua's admonition to the children of Israel in Joshua 1:8; take the Word of God as their authority, meditate on it and do what is written in the Word.

Do all the good you can, in all the ways you can, in all the places you can, at all the times you can, through all the people you can, as long as ever you can.

John Wesley

WHAT WE LEARNED

❑ Everyone has a story. Resolve to "write" the story of your life, with God's help, in such a way that you will have as few regrets as possible.

❑ Step out in faith for God. "Find a need and fill it."

❑ The Word of God is changeless. It has power to change lives, including mine.

What I Learned

_____
_____
_____
_____
_____
_____
_____
_____
_____
_____
_____

I'll Walk It Out By . . .

_____
_____
_____
_____
_____
_____
_____
_____
_____
_____
_____
_____

Part IV

THE REST OF
THE STORY . . .

EIGHTEEN

God's moral character is unchanging, and these moral principles (the Ten Commandments) have universal applications. . . . This commandment (the fifth) clearly indicates that God is a God who values relationships and holds them sacred. Furthermore, this mandate emphasizes that God is the designer of the home.

Dr. W. A. Criswell in *The Criswell Study Bible notes*

HOW YOU MAKE A MAN OUT OF A BOY

Honor thy father and thy mother....
Exodus 20:12a

How do you make a man out of a boy? Many stories of men who have achieved greatness have come out of the heartland of America. Garry Kinder's story traces its origins to the community of Pekin, Illinois, and to his parents, Jack and Edythe Kinder. The community of Pekin came into existence about 1824 when its first settler built a log cabin high on the east bank overlooking the Illinois River. The colorful history of the community reveals the transformation from a frontier outpost to a prosperous town with many people of German descent.

Pekin, in the second decade of the twentieth century, was a thriving small city of businesses and major industry. One such business was the Keystone Steel and Wire Company in nearby Bartonville where Garry's father Jack Kinder, Sr., worked. Edythe Lauterbach worked in the office at Keystone where she met her husband-to-be Jack Kinder, who was working in the fence shop at the time. Their courtship, however, was to go on for six years before she consented to marry the hardworking young man. Their marriage was celebrated on August 16, 1924 at St. Paul's United Church of Christ in Pekin.

The Formative Years

Into the latter part of the Great Depression, Jack Kinder, Jr., arrived on the scene, to be followed five years later, on May 22, 1933, by brother Garry. Garry says of his brother, "Jack and I have been bonded together from the very beginning; in fact, he knew me nine months before anybody else!" Jack was there when his parents were talking about this child who was to become a part of their family. The day would come when Jack would take that little fellow by the hand and introduce him to the big, wide world. Together they would do the fun things that boys, as brothers, do. They might even disagree about things now and then, as siblings are apt to do, but together they would experience the discipline and teachings of their mother and father; they would play and pray; learn and grow.

"There are dim, fuzzy memories of Mom tucking us in every night; of her bundling us up to play ball in Ubben's Field and always being available for the basement basketball games to even the sides," Garry says. "We remember Mom rising early in the morning to pack Dad's lunch, the double boiler full of oatmeal for breakfast, and the school lunches she prepared, often with a special treat. We remember, too, how she so often helped us solve our difficulties and fights, without taking sides, and keeping us in strong support of each other."

The brothers are often asked how they have gotten along so well through the years. Garry answers, "Well, we had a very harmonious family life. We've had our normal differences and as young boys growing up we would fist fight and wrestle all the time, but never with anger. Also, we're both very thick-skinned, so we could talk fairly tough to each other and even to the point of being mad, but then we'd walk away and forget it and keep going."

There are many pictures included in this book of the brothers' early childhood. One of them shows Garry in the midst of a group of basketball players who in 1947 won the state eighth grade basketball tournament. Garry relates, "This same group of athletes became the first state champions in the history of Pekin. We won the state Junior Legion Baseball Tournament with Jack as coach. I was the catcher and captain of the team. We went on to the national finals where we were beaten one game before the Junior Legion World Series. What great memories!"

Pekin High School

Each attended Pekin Community High School where they were members of the National Honor Society. They participated in three sports — baseball, basketball and football. Jack was All-State in basketball and Garry was All-State in baseball. Garry relates: "The same athletes [from Junior High School] won the state high school baseball championship in May 1951. A few weeks later I graduated from high school, and felt good about having collected nine varsity letters and having played on two state championship baseball teams. In July 1951, I played in the North-South All-Star Football Game. I was one of the quarterbacks for the South in a game where the North team, heavily dominated by Chicago players was favored. However, we ended up beating the North by two touchdowns.

"Later in the fall of 1951, I enrolled at Illinois Wesleyan University where I was the backup quarterback as a freshman for the first undefeated football team in the school's history. I was one of three freshmen who lettered on the varsity team that year. All in all, the year 1951 was filled with big events," he reminisces.

Both brothers worked hard at athletics and they excelled. They learned about sportsmanship, rules and fair play — needful disciplines they would carry with them forever. Garry remembers gratefully, "Mom and Dad always found the time to be at our ball games."

Each benefited from the wisdom of their parents, and from their instruction. Wise sayings were intertwined in the daily conversation of this mother and father; precept upon precept fell on listening ears and into hearing hearts. They were good listeners — listening to learn — developing empathy and respect for the opinions of others.

Parental Principles

The work ethic was clearly defined by the example of their father. "Our dad taught us to work, taught us discipline, and taught us to tithe ten percent and to save ten percent. These same values were to be taught later to our children. My daughters, Karen and Karol, practice this philosophy to this day and have even taught it to their children." This meant that God was to receive ten percent. These parental principles were enforced. The sons learned the lessons that came from giving with a cheerful heart in the German/Dutch church they attended as a family. "Rain, sleet or snow, we were in church. No exceptions were allowed," they recall.

Their background also brought strict discipline into their lives. As an example, at an early age Garry seriously injured his arm and the doctor said that he might end up having a stiff arm. "I was twelve years old and I caught my arm in a door handle, riding a bicycle, and it ripped all the blood vessels in my right arm. Luckily, I was about three or four doors from home. I got home and Mom put a tourniquet on it real quick and headed for the doctor.

"The doctor said I would have a stiff arm. Upon hearing this, Mom said to the doctor, 'Don't you ever talk like that in front of my son again. He will not have a stiff arm. I'll see to it that he doesn't.' She did this by forcing me to exercise and stretch the arm twice a day for three months to prevent it from getting stiff. That was bloody murder! Every time she did it, she said, 'That arm's going to put you through college. It's going to let you throw baseballs and footballs'." Garry was introduced to what can happen when one doesn't give up and give in to that which is difficult and painful. By the way, today, he doesn't have a stiff arm.

"You Must Be Born Again"

When Garry was sixteen and walking across the football field he found a tract lying on the ground. It was titled, "You Must Be Born Again." He explains the impact this had on him: "I'd gone to Sunday school every Sunday. I had never missed one Sunday in all my sixteen years. My Mom and Dad wouldn't allow us to miss for any reason. For instance, if we took a vacation, we'd go to Sunday school and get a note saying that we had attended there and we would take it back to our church. They kept track with a star every time you were there. If you had fifty-two of them — one for every Sunday in the year — you were a real winner. So I had that kind of Sunday school background. I was confirmed in a Confirmation Class. I did all of that. But I had never had a born again experience until I found the tract.

"I took it home, went into my bedroom, read it and prayed the prayer that was printed there, which was the sinner's prayer. That's why I'm so sold on the use of Gospel tracts." And that day, Garry Kinder became born again.

Illinois Wesleyan University

The Kinder brothers went to Illinois Wesleyan University where they again participated in three sports. Jack became an outstanding college basketball player. An injury to his left wrist cut Garry's athletic career short in the first football game of his sophomore year. "My parents took me to the Mayo Clinic in Rochester, Minnesota, in the hopes that they would give me some good news. They told me at age nineteen that my competitive athletic career was finished. From that point on I concentrated on fraternity and academic affairs, as well as, getting prepared as a college intern to sell insurance for The Equitable upon graduation.

"In my junior year, I was president of the Phi Gamma Delta fraternity. I was also a member of the Blue Key National Honor Society, which recognizes college seniors for their academic and leadership roles. In 1955, I graduated from Illinois Wesleyan and entered the life insurance business immediately."

Self-discipline, imagination, and staying power fueled their efforts as they became peak performers. Not only had they become high achievers, they were men of integrity.

The Million Dollar Round Table (MDRT)

Both brothers were good salesmen. They qualified for the Million Dollar Round Table at young ages, as well as being qualifying members for the 2001 MDRT in Toronto. They have conducted workshops at the MDRT conventions in Orlando and Toronto.

In 1976, Jack and Garry formed Kinder Brothers International, building in-depth training programs for more than three hundred companies, domestically and internationally. This has kept the brothers challenged as needs are brought to their attention and they seek ways to fill those needs. They have sponsored training programs with MDRT and the General Agents and Managers Association (GAMA) and they are recognized leaders in the development of interactive CD-ROM training.

They believe in the balanced life. They point to a concept developed by Dr. George W. Crane, a professor at Northwestern University, who says that each person carries throughout his and her career a "Cross of Life." *This cross has five dimensions — professional, physical, financial, personal, and spiritual. When these elements are in balance, a person can function at full capacity.* Dr. Crane feels that many people fail for reasons that have nothing to do with the way they perform their jobs. He said, *"They simply get the 'Cross of Life' out of balance."* The Kinder brothers' *Cross of Life* is in balance.

They try to communicate biblical philosophies that work 24/7, not just on Sunday. As he seeks to motivate others in the business world, here's what Garry says, "Live a life that attracts quality people to your organization. Once attracted, you should act and live a management life that will inspire and motivate people to higher levels of excellence. And when you do, you receive the greatest thrill that can come to anybody in the business world today."

Sermons We See

At business seminars, Garry often quotes the words of the poem *"Sermons We See,"* by Edgar Guest. He also uses it at least once a year at the Bible study to make the important point that people need to get on the racetrack.

The poem goes like this:

I'd rather see a sermon than hear one any day;
I'd rather one should walk with me than merely tell the way.

The eye's a better pupil and more willing than the ear,
Fine counsel is confusing, but example's always clear;
And the best of all the preachers are the men who live their creeds,
For to see good put in action is what everybody needs.
I soon can learn to do it if you'll let me see it done;
I can watch your hands in action, but your tongue too fast may run.
And the lecture you deliver may be very wise and true,
But I'd rather get my lessons by observing what you do;
For I might misunderstand you and the high advice you give,
But there's no misunderstanding how you act and how you live.

That poem itself describes the man Garry Kinder and is representative of what the world is looking for from those of us who claim to know Christ.

WHAT WE LEARNED

☐ The fifth commandment, to honor one's father and mother, was practiced by Jack and Garry Kinder. This resulted in God's wisdom being imparted to these brothers by their parents and it has borne fruit throughout their lives.

☐ The Bible says there are rewards in faithfulness. (See Psalm 128.) The habit of tithing, and loving and serving God were all things Garry learned in his formative years.

☐ People would rather see a sermon than hear one, any day.

What I Learned

_____

_____

_____

_____

_____

_____

_____

_____

_____

_____

I'll Walk It Out By . . .

_____

_____

_____

_____

_____

_____

_____

_____

_____

_____

_____

═══ NINETEEN ═══

Love has a locale here on earth and it is called the home. Home is where love is nourished, where it is best expressed. Out of the home all other relationships are influenced.

Mary Crowley in *Women Who Win*[1]

TWO DAUGHTERS
SPEAK THEIR HEARTS

The just [righteous] man walks in his integrity;
his children are blessed after him.
Proverbs 20:7

Garry Kinder's daughters, Karen and Karol, born thirteen months apart, speak with love and justifiable pride about their father. They spent the preschool years of their lives in Bloomington, Illinois. Then Garry moved his family to Akron, Ohio. Karen recalls her kindergarten through third grade years as being there. They next moved to Detroit, Michigan, which was short-lived, only for a year. "I was entering fifth grade when we moved to Dallas," Karen says.

"I'm always made to feel special by the people in the Bible study simply because I'm Garry's daughter. That tells you how highly they regard him. I see how people benefit from his teaching and leadership. And that tells you how much God is using him.

"Dad genuinely cares about people—although he's very tough-minded (as the history of his life will show)—but he has a very merciful side. He is always giving people the benefit of the doubt (to his detriment in some business dealings perhaps). Nevertheless, he has a very sharp business mind.

"I was shy, but a tough kid to raise—I am very stubborn, strong-headed. But he was tough with us, especially me. Actually, fear of Dad kept us out of lots of trouble! Yet he was very sympathetic to our hurts (breakups, disappointments). He cheered our successes and encouraged us to always try and do our best. He roughhoused with us as kids, and was a lot of fun. He tried to teach us golf (and didn't succeed at that)! We did get to travel to fun places with him and Mother on some of his business trips. The popular thing for teenagers was to go to Padre Island on spring break, but he would plan Hawaii trips for that time. That was a smart thing to do.

"Growing up with someone like Dad, you met a lot of well-known people and famous athletes, but we got used to not being intimidated by big names.

"One of the greatest things he did for us was to trust us (even more than I wanted to be trusted sometimes). He expected more from us and tried to give us responsibility much earlier than Mom would have liked. Examples would be getting jobs, staying out, driving places and working around the house.

"I had a lot of friends growing up, including some boyfriends, but they were all a little scared of Dad—he was a tough guy, maybe a little intimidating.

"I remember when I first got my driver's permit, he wanted to go right up onto LBJ [one of the busiest freeways in the greater Dallas area]. And that's what we did! I thought it was great! Among other things, I also inherited his driving style!"

Upon graduation from high school, Karen went to college at Baylor University in Waco, Texas. "After college, I went straight to work for a CPA firm. I kept taking the CPA test until I passed it. Then I went to work for a public accounting firm, which you had to do to fulfill part of the CPA requirements. (You have to pass the test and work a certain amount of hours in public accounting.) But Dad kept asking me to come to work for him. He and his brother had started Kinder Brothers and they had grown to the point where they needed a full-time accountant. It was in 1983 that I started working for him.

"I inherited Dad's good math mind. He is incredible as far as that goes. I became Kinder Brothers' first full-time comptroller. Dad could always tell at first glance if the monthly statement was off. He was instinctive about it (as if the numbers were all in his head and all he needed was a computer for us to print them out for the record). He was always right, but of course I always had a good explanation!

"I met my husband, David Smith, at Northwest Bible Church at a singles' retreat. When we started dating, we quit going to the singles' class and started going out to Dad's Bible study for our early Sunday morning class. We did this through our dating and engagement. We always felt very comfortable going to Dad's class and thoroughly enjoyed it. Dad is just a great teacher! Often we talked about how much we were getting out of that class and his teaching.

"Mom loved David. She saw her long years of prayers answered and we had a wonderful time planning the wedding. Dr. Criswell and David's brother, who is a preacher, married us on December 30, 1989, at Dallas First Baptist. Here's a funny memory—Dad and I were standing behind the fancy doors leading into the church, waiting to go down the aisle. The music stopped and then the hour started chiming. It stopped at eleven. I said to him, 'Dad, it's supposed to go to twelve.' But we were both beaming as we made our way down the aisle, arm in arm. I think he was happy to see his thirty-year-old daughter finally find someone who met his requirements!

"My sister Karol was my matron of honor; she was already married and had two children. Little Joy Elizabeth, her two-year-old at the time, appears in the video of the wedding, just an adorable little girl. Her other daughter, Grace Ann, would have been a flower girl, but she was very sick that day.

"Mom was really excited about my new in-laws and was looking forward to the day when we would have children. We were living in a condo and anticipating the day when we could buy our first home.

"Mom's sudden death in October 1990 brought a lot of changes into our lives. I was expecting our first child at the time and we had moved in with Dad. So we brought baby Lauren home to his house. It brought him such joy! It was really something. He became a wonderful grandpa!

"Mom was attractive, about 5'3", trim and always looked very well put together. She didn't spend a lot of money on herself; never wanted to go to the beauty parlor every week and have her hair done, so she found hairstyles that she could just do herself and she prided herself on that. She was the type of person who didn't feel like she needed to be pampered. She and I had a lot of the same taste in clothes and could even share clothes at times. We were both on the artistic side—music and art. Mom would always play music around the house.

"While she was a Bible Study Fellowship substitute leader, teaching was not her main gift. In fact, she felt uncomfortable with it. She and I are a lot alike in that respect—we don't get a big thrill out of getting up front and being a speaker. So that was tough for her, but she was willing and she did it. She enjoyed the preparation when she had to substitute, but her gift was administration, which she did very well for a long time. She took the BSF training, which qualified her to be a substitute. So she was a combination of administrative and could then step in and be a substitute. But she trusted God and her faith grew. I saw it. She really changed just from relying on the Lord over a period of ten years. It began while I was in college and obviously was going on right up until her death. She was very modest and had a servant's heart."

Mary Crowley used to say that the successful parent works himself out of the job of parenting, but never out of the relationship. The kindest thing we can do for our children is to teach them to be independent of us, as parents—but dependent on the Lord. Garry's daughters married and established Christian homes.

Garry's youngest daughter, Karol, speaks her heart: "Dad impacted our lives in a tremendous way. He truly helped us look at things with wisdom; he helped us become better, not bitter, about events that were disappointing or hurtful.

"I was in fourth grade when we moved to Dallas. I was very excited about moving to Texas. I pictured it as tumbleweeds, cowboys and Indians. I didn't know what it was all about because we'd lived in the mid-west. So coming down here was a big move for our family, but it was also very exciting. Dad had taken on this new responsibility and we were excited to have a pool in the backyard of our home. We enjoyed the warm weather as opposed to the colder northern climate. We acclimated to Dallas very well.

"Dad helped us look at opportunities and set goals. I'll never forget that on January 1 he would come into our rooms and say, 'OK, time to get up and set goals.' He would be so excited about the new year, forgetting the old and moving in with the new, moving on toward positive goals. I learned how to set goals and look forward and to think 'What can God do through the coming years?' He truly set us in a positive direction. Dad made a positive impact in our lives growing up, and he still does today.

"Another memory of growing up with Dad was how he would gather us together for family meetings on Sunday evenings. I have to admit that many times when I had other things I needed to do, or homework, or things I *wanted* to do, I would think 'I don't want to go to the family meeting. I don't have time for this.' But always it was a blessing. Dad would compliment us in our talents or abilities, or he would teach us from the Bible! Sometimes he would encourage us in some way and help us in going on in a better direction. I'm thankful for the lasting lessons he gave us in those meetings.

"College was a wonderful experience. Many of the friends we grew up with at First Baptist Dallas were there at Baylor University in Waco. First Baptist made a huge impact on my life, and I know on the lives of those close friends. I majored in Elementary Education earning a Bachelor of Science degree.

"Baylor is where I met my husband, Curt Ladd. We were in a small Bible study at the apartment complex. We began dating because we both had an interest in running. I was training for a marathon, and he had a growing interest in running, so he began running with me. We would go out and run seven to ten miles at a time, and we just enjoyed that training together. When I came up to Dallas to run the White Rock Marathon, he came and ran part of the way with me. That was an epoch in my life and my entire family came out to watch and hold up signs. Mom had made signs that said, 'I can do all things through Christ who strengthens me.' It was a beautiful experience to have them cheering me on. Dad even got in the race and ran it with me for a little bit. The encouragement I felt in that race was incredible. I was nineteen. I didn't run it to win; I ran it to finish — a marathon is 26.2 miles. Unless you're an incredible runner, you just run to achieve the goal of finishing. It took around 4 hours and 32 minutes.

"Today, I run occasionally — my knees are not as happy with me running. Dad, Curt, our daughters Grace and Joy, and I all ran the Turkey Trot in 2001. Because our girls love to run, we've decided we're going to make that a tradition, it's just 3.2 miles. Most cities have a Turkey Trot, and so does Dallas. Back when I was training for the marathon, I ran the 8-mile run, no big deal. Now it's a challenge to run the 3-mile.

"I was twenty-two when I married. Curt and I dated throughout my junior and senior years. He was graduating with his master's degree, and I with my undergrad. Dr. Criswell married us in the summer of 1982. It was a big, beautiful wedding, carefully planned by my mother. We came to Dallas to establish our home. Curt is from Memphis, born and raised there, but he chose Dallas. He loves my family. He loved my mother. Dad became a mentor to him.

"Curt thought he wanted to go into Christian psychology to become a counselor, but as he was looking into doctoral programs, after he'd finished his master's, Dad sat Curt down at the kitchen table. He said, 'Curt, I want to talk to you about the direction of your career.' He laid out to him the positives of a career in insurance as an agent. Curt had been in sales in several different ways. Twice, as a summer job he'd sold cemetery plots. If you can sell cemetery plots, you can pretty much sell anything. Curt had a strong sense about sales and was very gifted in that area. He wasn't the type who was bothered when someone said no. He just moved on. He was tough-skinned and was able to go into sales quite easily. Curt shifted directions from that day at the kitchen table and made the decision to go into insurance sales. Dad helped him get set up with a man he was quite familiar with and Curt stuck with it. He learned a lot from Dad. Dad is a teacher to insurance managers, so Curt's early training came from Dad. All the skills that Dad teaches agents, he poured into Curt and I think that has contributed greatly to make my husband the success he is today. Now Curt has taken all his knowledge as a life insurance salesman and has applied it to being a financial planner and helping people with their investments and planning their financial needs.

"We have two precious daughters, Grace and Joy. Mom often talked about what a glorious gift it was to be a grand-mother. She would say this was her second chance. Now she was a wonderful mother, yet she so humbly felt like there were many mistakes she made. Of course every mother feels that way. But she devoted her heart, her time, her life to her grandchil-dren. She was the most loving of grandmothers. She was always attentive and smiling, truly an encouragement to her grand-daughters. She adored them.

"Dad became a wonderful grandfather. I saw a new side emerge in him when he became a grandfather—a more caring, nurturing side that seemed to grow out of the experience of being a grandfather.

"As with most men, they are business building, and right-ly so for their families. And Dad did make this great impact on our lives as we were growing up, but it's interesting, as he grew older in years that the nurturing and emotional side of him came out, especially with the grandchildren. He constantly has us over and teaches them; he enjoys teaching with the whole fami-ly gathered around him. He and Janet love to have us come over on Sundays, at least twice a month. We will gather at their home for lunch either after church or in the evening."

Karol Ladd is a prolific young author of twelve books (and counting). In high school she enjoyed writing her thoughts con-cerning biblical matters. "Little essays," she calls them. She put them into files and her mother actually borrowed them from time to time for her teaching with Bible Study Fellowship. "I remember once she was teaching a Bible study on scripture memory and she asked for my file on that subject. She used all the material that I had pulled together. In a way, that was quite a compliment to me that she would want to use my material. So I think she knew I enjoyed thinking through issues and writing, but I don't think she knew I had an aspiration to be a writer at that point. She knew that I enjoyed speaking to groups and teaching Bible studies. I taught several neighborhood Bible studies and she would baby-sit the kids, making it possible for me to fulfill that desire and what God had put into my life. She was very supportive.

"When I was first published in 1994, it brought a smile to Dad's face. It may have made him think that I was possibly following in his footsteps. His writing is what motivated me to write books. I realized that if my dad could do it, so could I. God could allow me to write books, as well."

Karol's book, *The Power of a Positive Mom* (Howard Publishing, 2001) reached best-seller status almost immediately in the Christian Booksellers Association market. "It's done well by God's grace," she modestly states. "It's a God-thing," she adds.

"Even now, as to what I do as a writer, speaker, wife and mother, I feel like my dad was truly my inspiration. He was the one whose positive attitude, example, and leadership influenced me to reach greater heights. He was an example. He showed me the way. From him I've learned how to be a better speaker as well. In fact, sometimes when I'm speaking in front of an audience I think to myself, '*I sound just like Dad!*' People will come up to me afterwards and say I'm a great speaker, but I know it's because I've had great training. I watched and learned from him. I suppose that's truly what wore off on me."

Howard Hendricks, Distinguished Professor and Chairman of the Center for Christian Leadership at Dallas Theological Seminary, has often been heard to say, "Heaven help the home!" It can be said with certainty that heaven did help the Kinders in their establishment of a Christian home and in their parenting. Daughters who speak from their hearts about their parents such as Karen and Karol have done provide evidence that their home was a refuge — a place of peace, harmony, and beauty, a place where love was expressed. [Throughout this book, I have closed each chapter with a section called, **What We Learned,** based on what Garry does each Sunday in the Bent Tree Bible Study. For this chapter, I have chosen to use Karol Ladd's four words to remember.]

On the occasion of the "Champion for Christ" dinner and celebration for Garry Kinder, among the letters provided in the memory book, were two from his daughters.

Dear Dad:

As a father, you put some fear in us that kept us in line and yet you had a real soft heart when we were hurting. You always kept us positive and looking ahead. And, there are few people in the world who are so reliable and honest.

I am thankful for such a great dad and proud of such a great man!

Love,
Karen

To Dad:

I suppose it would be nearly impossible to put into words all that you mean to us. I am eternally thankful for the valuable lessons that you have poured into our lives. Not only am I blessed to have a father such as you, but Curt and the girls are fortunate as well. Under your leadership in this family, we have a foundation built on God's Word and fine example. Although I could choose hundreds of words to describe the influence that you have in our lives, I have chosen four with which to commend you on this page.

Love,
Karol

WHAT WE LEARNED

☐ Leadership: As a gifted leader you have been committed foremost in leading your family members to lives of responsibility to both God and man. You have led us faithfully through your example and instruction. You have taught us how to carefully, wisely and faithfully lead others so that your leadership has had a multiplying effect. Not everyone is qualified to be a leader, for leadership commands respect, integrity, responsibility and wisdom. Your leadership is characterized by all of these.

"For thou art my rock and my fortress; For Thy name's
sake Thou wilt lead me and guide me."
Psalm 31:3

☐ Character: There has never been a question as to your character or integrity. You are a man who can be trusted. Your word is good and your actions are upright. People can look to Garry Kinder and see God's goodness in action. Good character is not bought or proclaimed by one's self, but it is earned through a life of consistent living. I am grateful for your years of consistent living within our home, in the church and in the community.

"Blessed are those who hunger and thirst for
righteousness; for they shall be satisfied."
Matthew 5:6

❏ <u>Diligence:</u> "Never, never, never . . . give up." One of your favorite quotes from one of your favorite people, Winston Churchill. You taught us diligence. When the going gets tough, you taught us to persevere. You showed us through your example to keep on praying, working and growing through each experience that life brings. Recently life has brought some sad moments, and I have watched you grow in grace from each of these difficulties.

"Now for this very reason also, applying all diligence, in your faith supply moral excellence, and in your moral excellence, knowledge, and in your knowledge, self-control, and in your self-control, perseverance, and in your perseverance, godliness."
2 Peter 1:5,6

❏ <u>Godliness:</u> Your love for our Lord and His word characterize your life purpose. You find your wisdom, direction, encour-agement and hope from Him. I not only see in you a knowl-edge of His word, but a daily application and a heart for God. God is your strength, and you have led us as a fami-ly to that truth. Your faith will be passed down from gener-ation to generation, glorifying the Father.

What I Learned

_____

_____

_____

_____

_____

_____

_____

_____

_____

_____

_____

_____

I'll Walk It Out By . . .

_____

_____

_____

_____

_____

_____

_____

_____

_____

_____

_____

_____

_____

TWENTY

Having come in vital contact with Christ for themselves, John at once thought of his brother, and Andrew thought of his brother. . . . Let us seek to emulate these men. . . . Every believer is called to be a representative of Christ, to go to men and women with this message, "We have found Jesus, the Savior of sinners, who meets every need of the lost and the undone."

H. A. Ironside, Litt. D in *Addresses on the Gospel of John*[1]

A Brother Speaks His Heart

He first findeth his own brother. . . .
John 1:41a

"To the child of God, there is no such thing as accident. He travels an appointed way," wrote A. W. Tozer in, *We Travel an Appointed Way*. The person of true faith believes that God orders each life, that it is a journey ordered by the "secret script of God's hidden providence." [2]

No happenstance, no chance or mischance, brought Jack and Garry Kinder into the same home. Planned by God, their lives intertwined from birth, these two brothers have experienced God's providential care.

On the occasion of the event honoring Garry Kinder and his work with the Bent Tree Bible Study, many friends, co-workers, celebrities from the Christian world, and family members were given opportunities to speak their heart. Jack Kinder, five years Garry's senior, shared a story that was very timely and made a great point. The story speaks for itself of the esteem and love two brothers had each for the other.

"Back in the fifteenth century, there was a family growing up together in a little village outside of Nuremberg, Germany. It was a family of fifteen children. The father was working three jobs, just to keep food on the table for this hungry tribe. The two older children were boys, and they had an ambition and they shared the same dream. They wanted to someday find a way to get their education at the famous academy in Nuremberg, Germany.

"They were smart enough to know that their father was never going to be able to foot the bill, not even to get one of them through that education. So they made a pact. They were very close, had similar interests, similar ambitions, and similar names. They agreed that they would flip a coin in the air, and when it came down there would be a winner and a loser. 'The winner will go to the academy,' they agreed, 'and the loser will go down into the mines.' With his pay, the loser would finance the education of the winner. 'In four years, we will shift places. The other will get to go on to the academy. In eight years, we've both got our degrees.'

"So they flipped that coin into the air, and Albrecht Durer was the winner. Albert—similar name—was the loser. Albert went down into the mines. Albrecht went on to the academy where his carvings, his line drawings, his engravings, his wood cuts were an instant sensation. His work was the talk of the school. It was said that he was even better than the professors were. In four years, he graduated.

"The family gathered together around the table to celebrate this great event. They placed Albrecht at one end and Albert at the other. Albrecht rose as they began, and with a glass in his hand, he offered a toast: 'My dear brother, I am so indebted to you for what you've done to finance my education through the university. Now this toast is to you for all of the work and effort you have put forth. But it is also a toast to wish you well, for now it is your time to go to the academy.'

"All eyes shifted to the other end of the table. There was Albert, looking down at his hands, shaking his head. 'No, no. No,' he said. 'My dear brother, I love you, but look at these hands. Every finger has been broken in the work in the mine. I have arthritis so badly I can't even break the bread; I can't even cup the glass to return your nice toast. My dear brother, I love you, but the academy is not for me.'

"Four hundred years have passed since that toast was given to Albert. And they tell me in all the famous museums throughout the world hang the works, the creations of Albrecht Durer, but he's best known by you and me for his first creation. It is the painting he rendered of his brother's hands. Some of you have it on your walls, some wear it around their neck, we have it as bookends in our study at home. It is known as 'The Praying Hands'.

"The next time you look at that painting, look at it closely, and let it impress you with one thought—behind every great success story, and behind the success story of the Bent Tree Bible Study, is a common thread. And that thread is we all need each other. Tonight we've joined together to pay tribute to the spiritual leader, the catalyst, the teacher, and that's appropriate. But I remember another night, just less than two blocks outside the door of this building, where the Burns family invited a small group of Believers into their home. That was the meeting that gave birth to this Bible study, and out of that emerged what you celebrate here tonight.

"When we honor a great leader, a great human being, a great brother, a great teacher, like you have done here, we are in fact honoring ourselves. And so I congratulate not only my brother, I also congratulate each of you on the enormous impact that you've made and continue to make through the 'followship' that you display in following the great leader—Jesus Christ."

Some of Jack's final thoughts on his brother and the Bent Tree Bible Study—"It was 1980, the Bent Tree Country Club was the place; that's how it all got started. In almost a quarter of a century, many important things have taken place as a result of a few people stepping up and stepping out. From the bar of a posh country club, to women's Bible studies, to prayer ministries, to a counseling center, to the Roaring Lambs ministry, which is having a great impact on this nation—this is one modern-day story of the impact Jesus Christ can have through people who are *stepping up and stepping out!*"

> Inasmuch as ye have done it unto one of the least of these my brethren, ye have done it unto me.
>
> Matthew 25:40

WHAT WE LEARNED

☐ The power of praying hands and praying hearts.

☐ Family love and family devotion are beautiful to behold.

☐ There is one that sticketh closer than a brother—His name is Jesus Christ. (See Proverbs 18:24.)

What I Learned

_____
_____
_____
_____
_____
_____
_____
_____
_____
_____
_____
_____

I'll Walk It Out By . . .

_____
_____
_____
_____
_____
_____
_____
_____
_____
_____
_____
_____
_____
_____
_____

What I Learned

What I Want To Work On

Part V

FIGURATIVELY TAPPED ON THE SHOULDER . . . JUST DO IT!

Conclusion

Time To Step Up
and Step Out

As we come to the end of this book, I am prompted to share what God has put in my heart about *stepping up and stepping out.* . . . First of all, I was reminded of this quote:

> **To each there comes in their lifetime a special moment when they are figuratively tapped on the shoulder and offered the chance to do a very special thing, unique to them and fitted to their talents. What a tragedy if that moment finds them unprepared or unqualified for that which could have been their finest hour.**
>
> Sir Winston Churchill

Are you looking at your life—abilities—circumstances—knowing God is tapping you on the shoulder with an assignment? I found myself making a list of some very specific "nudges" I've gotten from God and hadn't, **until now,** acted on.

As I reflect back over the last twenty-two years that I've known Garry, and most of the people in this book, I am convicted in my spirit to acknowledge to myself, and God, the times I have not followed His nudge.

Many times, working for Garry, he has said to me, "Lu Ann, I don't have time to explain it right now. You'll have to trust me—just do exactly what I said—exactly like I said to do it. You'll understand later." Do you know, every single time he was right! I'm no theologian—but I am a follower of Christ—and I think God is asking all of us to "Trust Him, just do exactly what He says, exactly like He says to do it. You'll understand later. . . ."

We all know people or ministries like you have read about on these pages that have tremendously impacted our lives, met a need, given us courage, ministered when we were sick, helped us through grief, introduced us to our merciful Savior, Jesus Christ—on and on the list could go.

To me, one of the greatest things about being a Christian is that God sees every person as valuable and having something to contribute. He will eventually nudge us to *step up and step out in a particular area.*

John 12:35 says, "Walk while you have the light, lest darkness overtake you. . . ." Oswald Chambers writes in *My Utmost for His Highest*, "Beware of not acting upon what you see in your moments on the mountaintop with God." Our hope and prayer in writing this book is that more of you will act when that nudge from God comes—that you will act upon what you see in your moments on the mountaintop with God.

It's time to step up and step out—no questions asked—just do exactly what He says, exactly how He says to do it! We can trust the promise that Dr. Hawkins reminded us of in his inspiring introduction: "The steps of a good man are ordered by the Lord, and He delights in his way" Psalm 37:23.

May the Lord "order your steps," according to His Word.

Bent Tree Bible Study

Sample Lesson
(Taught by Garry Kinder)

14 Principles for Living the Christian Life

As I thought about today being Palm Sunday and thought about what message I might bring to you, I'm reminded that Christ came in on a donkey, Lord of lords and King of kings. They were honoring him . . . one week later they were crying, "Crucify him, crucify him." I was thinking about the impact that we need to have on lives of people for the cause of Christ.

Recently, I heard a pastor talk about the ten worst things Christ could ever say to you or to any individual. I don't think he'd say to anybody in this room, but what's the worst thing Christ could say to you? In Matthew 7:23 Jesus said, "Depart from me, I never knew you." That would be the worst thing anybody could have said to them by Christ. "Depart from me I never knew you." But, I cast out demons, I did this, I did that. "Depart from me, I never knew you."

The second worst thing that could be said of us, and I agree with the pastor, by the way, is found in John 7:6–7. His brothers, who did not believe in him at the time he was walking the earth, his own blood brothers said to him,

Why don't you go down to Jerusalem? Why don't you go down there and do your tricks? Why don't you go down there and heal the people? If you're so good why don't you go on down there? Jesus said, My time hasn't come yet. But you can go ahead.

Now the Living New Bible says it best. It's paraphrased this way: "Go on down there because you won't have any impact anyway." The second worst thing that anybody could hear from Christ is . . . you didn't have any impact. You didn't have any outreach. You didn't have an impact for Me. You sat there and you listened, but you never did much about it. That's the second worst thing that could be said to you and me.

Now having heard the man's message, it encouraged me and it inspired me to come up with ways we can have an impact. I started out with four or five, then it grew to six and seven. Finally, I ended up with fourteen ways out of the Bible that we can have an impact for Christ.

Please turn to Joshua. In Joshua chapter 1, verses 1-5, we read,

After the death of Moses, it came to pass that the Lord spoke unto Joshua, the son of Nun. 'Moses my servant is dead. Now therefore rise, go over to this Jordan, thou and all of his people, into the land I do give unto thee and all the children of Israel. Every place that the sole of your feet shall trod upon, that have I given unto you as I said unto Moses. From the wilderness, from this Lebanon all the way to the great river, the river Euphrates, all the land of the Hittites unto the great sea toward the going down of the sun, shall be your coast. There shall not be any man able to stand before thee all the days of thy life. As I was with Moses, so I will be with thee. I will not fail thee. I will not forsake thee.'

Those are great words.

Now, listen to what he says to Joshua. He said Joshua, go over there across the river. Go over there; take over the land. I want you to have an impact. Now how are you going to have an impact?

Number one — be strong! "Be strong and of good courage. For unto these people shalt thou divide the inheritance of the land which I swear unto their fathers to give them." Now He repeats it again. This is God talking to Joshua, in his ear. "Only be thou strong, and very courageous that thou mayest observe to do according to all the law, which Moses my servant commanded thee. Turn not from it, from the right nor from the left, that thou mayest prosper wherever thou goest. This book of the law shall not depart out of thy mouth but thou shall meditate therein, day and night, that thou mayest observe to do according <u>to all</u>, to all that is written therein, for then thou shalt make thy way prosperous and then thou shall have good success. Have I not commanded thee? Be strong and of good courage. Be not afraid. Neither be thou dismayed. For the Lord thy God is with thee withersoever thou goest."

Fourteen ways to have an impact for Christ. The first four come out of Joshua, chapter one as we read them. What's the first one? Be strong! Be strong. Never take counsel of your fears. Don't be afraid. Be strong! Go in there and be strong. You can be strong. Number one, we can have an impact; we can be strong because we know from this Scripture that God is with us. The most powerful words ever uttered, God is with me. God is with me. Be strong!

The second way to have an impact is to banish fear and doubt — be courageous. Be courageous. Be bold! Banish fear and doubt. Number two, banish fear and doubt. Who would have you doubt? The devil! The devil would have us doubt. We are to be bold, not doubters. We're to be strong! Be bold! Be bold! Be courageous! Be brave!

In studying the messages of Peter and the early church, I'm amazed at the boldness of Peter. Peter was not politically correct. Peter was not seeker sensitive. Peter was bold! Peter said, "Repent." You know the first words out of his mouth when he stood up to preach, "Repent! You killed Jesus. Repent!"

Now you go back and read Acts, you'll find those words. I paraphrased them, but that's what he's saying. Repent, you killed Jesus. Repent. They threw him in jail. He says I can't stop talking. You can tell me what's of man, but I'm of God. Be bold!

My brother and I travel around the world. We just got back from Indonesia, Malaysia, Thailand and Singapore. Over there the church is on fire. The thing I noticed about that church compared to the church in this country is they're on fire and they're bold. They are bold, they are not politically correct. Now in many of those countries they can get thrown in jail for mentioning Christ's name. They are bold. You ought to see them; it's unbelievable. Stand around talking to them, they'll say, "This fellow here, he's got an alternate lifestyle." A Christian will speak up and say, "No, he's a sinner. He is a sinner. He has a sinful lifestyle. He is a sinner!!"

They say, "This man is a Buddhist." They say, "No, he's not a Buddhist. He's an idol worshipper. He worships idols." And they'll look him right in the eye and say, "You need Christ. You need Christ; you're worshipping idols. You need Christ." They're bold. They're bold to the extent they could be thrown in jail.

What's the point here? How do you have an impact for Christ? Be strong. Banish fear and doubt. Number two, be bold, be brave, be courageous — banish fear and doubt!

And the number three — He says pay attention to the law, observe to do according to all the law which Moses my servant commanded thee. All the law. Now, we've thrown the Ten Commandments out in America. We're throwing them out of the school; we're throwing them out of the public squares. We're throwing them out of the courthouse. But listen, the Ten Commandments are still good. Did Jesus come to destroy the law? No, he came to fulfill the law. The law is still valid. And what's that law? Honor God. Have no other God before me. No graven images. Never use the Lord's name in vain. Know the law, practice the law.

I've been in and out of the locker rooms, in and out of the country clubs, on and off the golf courses. I've heard profanity all my life. But the one that gets me is when somebody uses the name of the Lord in vain. It says right here explicitly, do not use the name of the Lord in vain.

Keep the Sabbath day. Honor your father and thy mother . . . all the days of their life . . . all the days of their life. Do not steal and do not cheat. Do not kill. Do not commit adultery. Do not give false witness. Do not covet. Hey, it's still good stuff! It's still needed. He said Joshua, you pay attention to the law, and don't you vary from it from the left or the right. Don't you vary from it at all. Don't turn to the right; don't turn to the left. You stay right with that law.

Then the fourth thing, God said to Joshua was, "Meditate in this book night and day." Meditate in this book night and day. That's why I'm grateful to Mrs. Criswell for encouraging me to read this book straight through once a year and to read Proverbs regularly. Meditate in here day and night, that thou mayest observe to do according to all that is written therein—to do according to all that is written therein. And one thing we have to remember in America is when the government condones what the Bible condemns; we have to stick with the Bible.

We cannot be doing what the government condones. Just because the government says it's all right, doesn't make it all right. We have to meditate in here day and night, so we can do according to all that is written therein. Now that's the first four, be strong, be courageous, keep the law and meditate in the book day and night. The next three come out of Proverbs.

Now Proverbs is a book that gives us discipline.

So the fifth way to have an impact for Christ is to live the disciplined life. Proverbs is all about discipline. Discipline your child. In fact, what does it say? Not very good today, paddle the child to keep him out of hell. Discipline your child. Discipline your life. Discipline your eating habits. Discipline, discipline, discipline! I like what Paul Harvey says about that, "a democracy without discipline isn't a democracy, it's chaos." And I love what Dr. Dobson says about it, "any religion without discipline isn't a religion." Discipline! Proverbs says discipline.

The next thing Proverbs says is with all thy getting, get wisdom. What is wisdom? With all thy getting, Solomon says, get wisdom. What is wisdom? Get wisdom! It's knowing the will of God for your life and doing it. Modern day secular people call it a mission statement. Have a mission statement for your life—what you want your life to stand for—a mission statement. Find God's will and do it!

Wisdom is having knowledge and applying it. Wisdom, knowledge . . . knowledge has never been power. Knowledge by itself is not power. The world is full of educated derelicts. Only knowledge that's used is power. We might know God's will for our life, but wisdom is knowing God's will for our life and doing it. Number six, get wisdom—know God's will for your life and do it.

The seventh principle for having an impact comes out of Proverbs 24:27. Prepare thy work without and make it fit for thyself in the field and afterward build thine house. Now here again, the Living New Bible paraphrases that verse. As you know, a man who wanted his twelve-year-old son to be able to understand it paraphrased the Living New Bible. The Living New Bible there says build your business before you build your house. Now we need to hear that in

America because young people are out trying to buy a house bigger than their parents, they mortgage to get a car, they're doing this and doing that, the clothes they wear, the gold they wear.

I mean, in America we get everything first, and then we don't have time to tithe; we can't tithe because our mortgage payment is too high. Can't tithe because of the credit cards. Can't tithe because of the money I'm paying for the last vacation. The Bible says build your business, then build your house. Americans need to hear that. Build your business, then your house. They get it mixed up. They want to build the house, buy the cars, take the vacation, do everything and then try to pay for it.

We grew up in Pekin, Illinois. Now that's in the heart of the corn country. Most of my family were farmers. My dad was not, but my grandpas and my uncles were farmers, and we'd go down farm roads. And as my dad would take us down a farm road he would say to us, "You can always tell a good farmer by looking at his barn. Look at his fences. Look at his tractors. Look at his animals. Don't look at his house, because the good farmer builds his barn first. Takes care of the fences, and the animals and the tractors and then takes care of his house." And we'd be going down a farm road and he'd say, "Take a look at that farm over there. See that barn, see how good his fence is. Look at his tractors. Look at his animals. Now his house is not all that much to look at, but he's taken care of his barn. He's taken care of his business." Now we go down the road a little further and he said, "Now look at this man. Look at his barn falling down. Fences are falling down. Look at his animals. Look at his house; he has a nice house. He's a poor farmer." That's what my dad would say. Well I don't know if my dad read that out of Proverbs or not, but Proverbs 4:27 says, build your business, then build your house. Number seven, if you want to have an impact build your business, take care of your employer, your employees. Build your business, then build your house.

Numbers eight, nine and ten I picked up over the years from Howard Hendricks. I like to listen to his tapes and read his material. One time I was listening to him talk about a young pastor that came to him and said, "Dr. Hendricks, I'm having trouble putting it all together. I'm torn between spending time with my family, spending time with my spouse, and spending time in my ministry. I'm torn. Could you help me?"

And Dr. Hendricks said to this young man something that I've always taken to heart. And again, Americans need to listen to this. He said, "If you want to take good care of your kids, the first thing to do is love their mother." Love their mother.

So, if you want to have an impact for Christ, the number eight thing I have listed here is love your spouse. Love your spouse. Do you know what kids need most ; they need to see loving parents. They need to see that their father loves their mother and their mother loves their father. Love your spouse. He said if you want to have an impact on your kids, love their mothers.

He also said, and this would be the ninth principle, "Be a role model for your children." Be a role model for your children, because if you're not, then the athlete will become the role model, the rock singer will become the role model. You be the role model for your kids. So I say to parents and grandparents all over the country and all over the world, be a role model for your kids.

Be highly successful in everything you do. We're taught in here in this Word, do everything as unto Christ, that includes your business, that includes your employment, do everything as unto Christ. Be a role model for your kids.

Then he told this young man, spend time alone. Be sure that you block out some time to be alone. He said you cannot be all things to all people if you're always around people. You have to get away from people. You have to have time alone, quiet time, prayer time. You know the devil would like to have you do everything except pray. He would like to have you do everything except pray and read the Bible. He'd like you to go to committee meetings, he'd like you to go do this and go do that, all surrounding the church. Just don't take time to pray and read the Bible. Don't take time to be alone. The devil would have us do everything but those two things.

Number ten, spend time alone. Now I don't know about you, but when I get ready to read the Bible, sometimes I'll sit there and read the Bible and five minutes later I'm on the same verse. Has that ever happened to you? Get ready to pray, and five minutes later say, now let's see, what was . . . I haven't said anything here yet. I haven't heard anything, I haven't said anything. He'd have us do everything but those two things. So, time alone, quiet time.

Then the 11th principle comes out of the book of James. In the book of James—you really don't need to turn to it because I'm not going to quote any scriptures directly except that the book of James says what? One of the main themes in the book of James is discipline your tongue. Discipline your tongue; be very careful of gossip. Be very careful of "they said." Did you hear about Pete? Did you hear about Mary? What'd you think of Joe? What'd you think of this? What do you think of that? Did you hear anything about that? Did you hear anything about this?

Discipline the tongue. You want to have an impact for Christ, discipline the tongue. One of the greatest thoughts I've heard over the years is, if you're going to talk about somebody make sure they're there when you're talking about them. Discipline the tongue.

The last three principles 12, 13 and 14 come out of Luke 17. Luke 17, verses 11 through 19. The last three principles I want to give you come right out of these verses. Luke, Chapter 17, 11–19.

And it came to pass as he went to Jerusalem that he passed through the midst of Samaria and Galilee. And as he entered into a certain village, there met him ten men that were lepers, which stood afar off. And they lifted up their voices and said 'Jesus, Master, have mercy on us.' And when he saw them he said unto them, 'go show yourselves unto the priest.' And it came to pass, that as they went they were cleansed. And one of them when he saw that he was healed turned back with a loud voice, with a loud voice, glorified God, fell down on his face at his feet giving him thanks, and he was a Samaritan. And Jesus answering said, 'were there not ten cleansed, but where are the other nine? There are not found any that returned to give glory to God save this stranger.' And he said to him, 'arise, go thy way, thy faith hath made thee whole.'

The 12th principle, the 13th principle, and the 14th principle that I'd like to share with you today come right out of these verses.

Number 12 . . . take all of your needs to Jesus. These lepers knew where to go. They were standing afar off but they hollered, "Jesus, Jesus, help us, cleanse us." They knew where to go. Take your needs to Christ. Want to have an impact for Christ? Take your needs to Christ. Big needs, medium-sized needs, small needs . . . take all your needs to Christ. Principle number 12, take all your needs to Jesus.

Principle number 13, do what he says. Do what he says. I've heard Mrs. Criswell say on many occasions, and I've also heard Dr. Criswell say many times, in the Old Testament God talked to Joshua right in his ear. . . he talked to Moses right in his ear . . . he talked to Elijah right in his ear. Today he talks to us through his Word, and through the power of the Holy Spirit. Whatever Jesus says to do . . . go do it. Every once in awhile, in fact more than every once in awhile, somebody will come to me and say, I'm thinking about doing this and doing this and I knew you would . . . have some

Christian insight. Just wanted to see what you think. They say, "I really believe God's telling me to do this." I say, no God's not telling you to do that. God will never tell you to do anything that goes against the book. And that goes against the book. He's never going to tell you to do that. He's not nudging you to do that. Somebody else is nudging you to do that. Don't go against the book. Go do what Jesus says to do.

It's very interesting in the Old Testament, Solomon said in Proverbs with all thy getting, get wisdom. Jesus comes along, and I'm paraphrasing now, Jesus says with all thy getting, get going. You know most of the time when he gives you instructions, it's almost always go. What'd he tell these people? Go! Go over there and see the priest. What did he tell the woman? Go! Go and sin no more. He told the people leading up to Palm Sunday, go get the donkey.

Even when he wants us to wait, like he told the disciples, go to Jerusalem and wait. Go! Generally his answer to us is to go do something. Get something done. Be on the move. Don't just sit there, do something. Go! Go! So whatever it is, we are to do what he says. If you read this carefully, there are a lot of instructions here on go. Go! Don't sit around; go. Go into the prisons with Bill Glass. Go witness. Go door knocking. Go! Go! Go! Go! That's number 13.

Number 14 I think becomes very obvious.

Number 14 is be thankful in all things. Take time every day to be thankful, for big blessings, small blessings. I don't know about you, but I get in a hurry, and I'm sure you do too, praying on the move. You know what I mean? God, I'm going to be very busy today so if you'll take care of these five things, I have to go. I have some things I have to work on. If you'll take care of those things over there, I'd really appreciate it. Next day, here's another list by the way. Here's a list for Tuesday. I forgot Monday. He did a good job Monday, but I forgot to tell him he did a good job. So we are to always go back and to be thankful.

Fourteen principles. Reviewing them again, the first one is be strong, banish fear and doubt. Number two, be courageous, be bold, be brave. Number three, follow the law. Jesus said I came not to destroy it but to fulfill it. Number four, read the book, meditate therein day and night. Number five, discipline your life. Number six, with all thy getting, get wisdom. Know God's will for your life and do it. Number seven, build your business before you build your house. Number eight, love your spouse. Number nine, be a role model for your children. Number ten, spend time alone. Number eleven, discipline your tongue, watch gossip. Number twelve, take your needs to Jesus. Thirteen, go do what he says. And fourteen, be thankful in all things.

We read Matthew 25:21, not the ten worst things that Jesus could say, but . . . what's the finest thing Jesus could say to us? What's the finest thing he could say? It is in Matthew 25:21. Matthew 25:21, "His lord said unto him, Well done thou good and faithful servant. Thou hast been faithful over a few things, I will make thee ruler over many things. Enter thou into the joy of thy lord." Greatest thing that Jesus could say to us is "enter in."

Greatest thing he says is you are a believer, your name is written into the book of life, enter in. The second greatest thing he could say to us is you had an impact. You had an impact. You were good with little things, I am now going to make you rule over many things. Have an impact.

My final message to you today would be . . . do it now. Don't put it off. Don't say when the time's right. Don't say, next month, next year. I'm gonna get some things in line and then I'm going to do it. You never know — life is short and life is fragile. For years I sat out where you're sitting. The last sixteen years I've been teaching and working in Bent Tree Bible Study on Sunday mornings. Life is short and life is fragile, you never know when tragedy's going to strike in your life or something's going to happen.

Seven and a half years ago I lost my wife of thirty-four years. Now here was a lady who'd never been sick a day in her life. She'd had the flu once at age twenty-four. She was in the hospital to bear two children. She was out walking on a Wednesday morning just before she was to get ready to teach and lecture at Bible Study Fellowship. She was out walking four miles for her health. She got back within two blocks of the house and a car goes through a stop sign and kills her. Instantly. Tragically. Life is short and life is fragile. There's just one of them. We never know. So if we're going to have an impact we better start today.

Now the pleasant side of that story is that six years ago this month, I met Janet. She lost her husband to cancer ten years ago. And five years ago this month, March 4, 1992, we were married. Dr. Criswell did the service, a private little marriage ceremony. Dr. Criswell said to us before that service something that I want to share with you. To me it is very powerful. Dr. Criswell said, talking about our spouses who were deceased, He said, "Your love for one person will never diminish your love for another. Love never divides. Love always multiplies. And what this world needs is more love."

The greatest commandment of all is what? Love God with all your heart, mind and soul. And commandment number two is like unto it, love your neighbor as yourself. Love . . . love . . . we should have such a love for Christ that we want to have an impact for him while we're here. Don't put it off, do it now.

Let's bow our heads in prayer. *Our heavenly Father, we thank you for this time. We thank you for your Word, for your Word is truth. We thank you for this Bible study, right here.*

Dear God, I thank you for everybody gathered here this morning. Bless every person here today. May we be determined, each one of us, to go out of here and have an impact for you — not for our glory, but your glory.

Dear God, at this time of the year, this Palm Sunday as we get ready to go into Easter week, we thank you for coming down and dying for us, shedding your blood for the remission of our sins. We thank you for rising again the third day and going to prepare a place for us, that where you are, we may go also. We thank you for those that have gone before us. We thank you for the power of the Holy Spirit that you have sent us to help us pray. He helps us read the Bible and He gives us the power and strength to have an impact for you.

May every word we utter and every step we take be always acceptable in thy sight, for it's in Christ's name we pray. Amen.

FOOTNOTES

Preface
[1] Mother Teresa, *One Heart Full of Love* (Ann Arbor, Michigan: Servant Books, 1984), 59.

[2] Oswald Chambers, *The Complete Works of Oswald Chambers* (Grand Rapids, MI: Discovery House Publishers, 2000) 272.

Chapter One
[1] Charles R. Swindoll, *Rise & Shine* (Portland, OR: Multnomah Press, 1989), 71.

Chapter Two
[1] Howard G. Hendricks, *Color Outside the Lines* (Nashville, TN: Word Publishers, 1998), 54.

Chapter Four
[1] Warren W. Wiersbe, *Be Obedient.* (Wheaton, IL: Victor Books)

Chapter Five
[1] Helen Hosier, *Jesus: Love in Action*, Chapter 7, "Jesus as the True Emancipator".

Chapter Six
[1] Dr. J. Vernon McGee, *Thru the Bible with J. Vernon McGee, Vol. V* (Nashville: Thomas Nelson Publishers, 1983), 317.

[2] Ibid., 317.

Chapter Seven
[1] Dale Evans Rogers, *The Woman at the Well* (Old Tappan, NJ: Fleming H. Revell Co., 1970), frontpiece material.

[2] Ibid., 72.

[3] Ibid., 72.

Chapter Nine
[1] Charles Stanley, *The Blessings of Brokenness* (Grand Rapids, MI: Zondervan Publishing House, 1997), 23, 24.

[2] Oswald Chambers, *My Utmost for His Highest* (New York: Dodd, Mead & Co., 1959), October 31 devotional, page 305. The devotional that Barbara Kinder had read on the day she graduated to glory.

[3] Charles Stanley, *The Blessings of Brokenness* (Grand Rapids, MI: Zondervan Publishing House, 1997), 59-61.

Chapter Ten
[1] *The Criswell Study Bible* (Nashville: Thomas Nelson Publishers, 1979), Criswell Center for Biblical Studies. Taken from notes on John 14.

Chapter Eleven
[1] As quoted in *Getting to the Other Side of Grief: Overcoming the Loss of a Spouse* by Susan J. Zonnebelt-Smeenge and Robert C. DeVries, pg. 99. Quoting Sidney Zisook and Stephen R. Shuchter, "Early Psychological Reaction to Stress of Widowhood," *Psychiatry 54* (November 1991): 320-32.

[2] Warren W. Wiersbe, *Be Obedient*, (Wheaton, IL: Victor Books), *128.*

[3] A. W. Tozer, *The Knowledge of the Holy* (New York: Harper & Brothers, 1961), 109.

Chapter Twelve
[1] S.D. Gordon, *Quiet Talks on Prayer* (New York: Grosset and Dunlap, 1904).

Chapter Thirteen
[1] Bob Briner, *Roaring Lambs* (Grand Rapids, MI: Zondervan Publishing House, 1992), 36, 37.

[2] Ibid., 28.

[3] Ibid., 177.

Chapter Fifteen
[1] *The Criswell Study Bible,* 815.

[2] Ibid., 1452.

Chapter Sixteen
[1] Ibid., 732.

[2] Warren W. Wiersbe, *The Integrity Crisis* (Nashville: Oliver Nelson, a Division of Thomas Nelson Publishers, 1988), 60.

[3] Ibid., 76.

[4] Ibid., 135.

Chapter Nineteen
[1] Mary C. Crowley, *Women Who Win* (Old Tappan, NJ: Fleming H. Revell Co., 1979), 63.

Chapter Twenty
[1] H. A. Ironside, Litt. D., *Addresses on the Gospel of John* (New York: Loizeaux Brothers, Inc., 1942), 65, 66.

[2] A. W. Tozer, *We Travel an Appointed Way* (Camp Hill, PA: Christian Publications, 1988), 1.

BIBLIOGRAPHY

Beamer, Lisa with Ken Abraham. *Let's Roll.* Wheaton, Illinois: Tyndale House Publishers, Inc., 2002.

Briner, Bob. *Roaring Lambs.* Grand Rapids, Michigan: Zondervan Publishing House, 1993.

Briner, Bob. *The Leadership Lessons of Jesus.* Nashville, Tennessee: Broadman & Holman Publishers, 1997.

Briner, Bob. *More Leadership Lessons of Jesus.* Nashville, Tennessee: Broadman & Holman Publishers, 1998.

Colson, Charles. *The God of Stones and Spiders.* Wheaton, Illinois: Crossway Books, 1990.

Colson, Charles. *Loving God.* Grand Rapids, Michigan: Zondervan Publishing House, 1983.

Colson, Charles. *Against the Night.* Ann Arbor, Michigan: Servant Publications, 1989.

Colson, Charles. *The Body: Being Light in Darkness.* Dallas, Texas: Word Publishing, 1992.

Covey, Stephen R. *Principled-Centered Leadership.* New York: Simon & Schuster, Inc., 1990.

Covey, Stephen R. *The 7 Habits of Highly Effective People.* New York: Simon & Schuster Inc., 1989.

Criswell, W.A. *Five Great Questions of the Bible.* Grand Rapids: Zondervan Publishing House, 1958.

Criswell, W.A. *Our Home In Heaven*. Grand Rapids: Zondervan Publishing House, 1964.

Criswell, W.A. *Why I Preach the Bible Is Literally True*. Nashville: Broadman Press, 1969.

Criswell, W.A. *The Scarlet Thread Through the Bible*. Nashville: Broadman Press, 1971.

Criswell, W.A. *What to Do Until Jesus Comes Back*. Nashville: Broadman Press, 1975.

Criswell, W.A. *Welcome Back Jesus!* Nashville: Broadman Press. 1976.

Criswell, W.A. *The Criswell Study Bible*. Nashville: Thomas Nelson Publishers, 1979.

Criswell, W.A. *Standing on the Promises*. Dallas: Word Publishing, 1990.

Criswell, W.A., Patterson, Paige. *Heaven*. Wheaton, Illinois: Tyndale House Publishers, 1991.

Criswell, W.A. *Messages from My Heart*. Baton Rouge, Louisiana: REL Publications, 1994.

Eldridge, John. *Wild at Heart*. Nashville, Tennessee: Thomas Nelson Publishers, 2001.

Farrar, Steve. *Finishing Strong*. Sisters, Oregon: Multnomah Books, 1995.

Glass, Bill. *Expect to Win*. Dallas, Texas: Bill Glass Ministries, 1998.

Glass, Bill. *How to Win When the Roof Caves In*. Grand Rapids, Michigan: Fleming H. Revell, 1988.

Glass, Bill, Pluto, Terry. *Crime: Our Second Vietnam*. Dallas, Texas: Bill Glass Ministries/Champions For Life, 1999.

Graham, Billy. *The Collected Works of Billy Graham*. New York, New York: Inspirational Press, 1975.

Graham, Billy. *Hope for the Troubled Heart*. Dallas, Texas: Word Publishing, 1991.

Graham, Billy. *Peace with God*. Dallas, Texas: Word Publishing, 1953.

Graham, Jack. *Lessons from the Heart*. Chicago, Illinois: Moody Press, 2001.

Hawkins, O.S. *Culture Shock*. Dallas, Texas: Annuity Board, 2002.

Hawkins, O.S. *Drawing the Net*. 2nd Printing, Dallas, Texas: Annuity Board, 2002.

Hawkins, O.S. *Great News for Great Days*. Dallas, Texas: Annuity Board, 2001.

Hawkins, O.S. *Rebuilding: It's Never Too Late for a New Beginning*. Dallas, Texas: Annuity Board, 1999.

Hawkins, O.S. *Moral Earthquakes and Secret Faults*. Nashville, Tennessee: Broadman & Holman Publishers, 1996.

Hendricks, Howard & Hendricks, William. *As Iron Sharpens Iron*. Chicago: Moody Press, 1995.

Hendricks, Howard. *Standing Together*. Gresham, Oregon: Vision House Publishing, Inc., 1995.

Hosier, Helen Kooiman. *100 Christians Who Changed the 20th Century*. Grand Rapids, Michigan: Fleming H. Revell, 2000.

Jackson, Richard. *Freedom is Never Free.* Nashville, Tennessee: Broadman Press, 1976.

Jackson, Richard. *How To's on the Highway to Heaven.* Phoenix, Arizona: Exposition Press, 1985.

Jackson, Richard. *The Pulpit of His Passion.* Phoenix, Arizona: Exposition Press, 1986.

Jackson, Richard. *The Covenant of God's Love (Soul-winning New Testament)* Soul-winning notes written by Richard Jackson. LaHabra, California: Lockman Foundation, 1999.

Ladd, Karol. *The Power of a Positive Mom.* West Monroe, Louisiana: Howard Publishing Co., Inc., 2001.

Ladd, Karol. *The Power of a Positive Woman.* West Monroe, Louisiana: Howard Publishing Co., Inc., 2002.

Ladd, Karol. *Table Talk.* Nashville, Tennessee: Broadman & Holman, 1999.

Ladd, Karol. *Scream Savers.* Nashville, Tennessee: Broadman & Holman, 1999.

Lucado, Max. *A Love Worth Giving.* Nashville, Tennessee: Thomas Nelson Publishers, 2002.

Lucado, Max. *God Came Near.* Sisters, Oregon: Multnomah Publishers, 1998.

Lucado, Max. *He Chose the Nails.* Nashville, Tennessee: Thomas Nelson, 2002.

Lucado, Max. *When Christ Comes.* W Publishing Group, 1999.

Lucado, Max. *When God Whispers Your Name.* Nelsonword Publishing Group, 1999.

MacArthur, John F. *The Gospel According to Jesus*. Grand Rapids, Michigan: Zondervan Publishing House, 1988.

MacArthur, John F. *The Vanishing Conscience*. Dallas, Texas: Word Publishing, 1994.

Mason, John. *An Enemy Called Average*. Tulsa, Oklahoma: Insight International, 1990.

Maxwell, John C. *Developing the Leader Within You*. Nashville, Tennessee: Thomas Nelson Publishers, 1993.

Maxwell, John C. *Leadership 101*. Tulsa, Oklahoma: Honor Books, 1994.

McCartney, Bill. *Sold Out: Becoming Man Enough to Make a Difference*. Nashville, Tennessee: Word Publishing, 1997.

Morley, Patrick M. *The Man in the Mirror*. Grand Rapids, Michigan: Zondervan Publishing House, 1989.

Teaff, Grant, Rice, Homer. *Lessons for Leaders*. Longstreet Press, 2000.

Warren, Rick. *The Purpose-Driven Church*. Grand Rapids: Zondervan, 1995.

Wilkinson, Bruce. *The Prayer of Jabez*. Sisters, Oregon: Multnomah Publishers, 2000.

Wilkinson, Bruce. *Secrets of the Vine*. Sisters, Oregon: Multnomah Publishers, 2001.

Wilkinson, Bruce. *A Life God Rewards*. Sisters, Oregon: Multnomah Publishers, 2002.

Yancey, Philip. *I Was Just Wondering*. Grand Rapids, Michigan: Wm. B. Eerdmans Publishing Co., 1989.

Yancey, Philip. *Disappointment with God: Three Questions No One Asks Aloud.* Grand Rapids, Michigan: Zondervan Publishing House, 1988.

CONTACT INFORMATION

Bent Tree Bible Study
17110 Dallas Parkway, Suite 220
Dallas, TX 75248

Phone: 972-380-0123